Sul H. Lee
Editor

D0196011

Improved Access to Information: Portals, Content Selection, and Digital Information

Improved Access to Information: Portals, Content Selection, and Digital Information has been co-published simultaneously as *Journal of Library Administration*, Volume 39, Number 4 2003.

Pre-publication
REVIEWS,
COMMENTARIES,
EVALUATIONS . . .

"**R**ICH AND VARIED. . . . Worth the read. Is knowledge management just a trend? Are portals passé? Does 'digital library' convey the richness and complexity of the current scholarly information environment? This collection will help you wrestle with these and other questions."

Mark Haslett, MLS
University Librarian
University of Waterloo Library
Ontario

More Pre-publication
REVIEWS, COMMENTARIES, EVALUATIONS . . .

"**H**IGHLY ENGAGING. . . . Nine well-known library leaders describe the challenges of improving access to electronic information. Their thoughts document and frame current practice, lay out the challenges of building and maintaining digital content, and pose significant questions to guide research agendas. Their wise minds also wrestle with the future of libraries. Digital content providers, information system and service practitioners, library and information science researchers, and campus computing visionaries will gain new perspective and appreciation for the enormous tasks already accomplished and the substantial intellectual, political, financial, and technical problems that remain. Those tasks will be a little easier, thanks to this book."

Maurita Peterson Holland, AMLS
Associate Professor
and Director
of Academic Research
School of Information
University of Michigan, Ann Arbor

"**T**his book CONTAINS VITAL IDEAS AND REFERS TO MANY INNOVATIVE APPROACHES for the practitioner to consider. . . . Presents the views and strategic information access improvement strategies of innovative leaders of library professional practice. . . . Addresses the issues and concerns of matching clients with the information resources they need in an enlightening and enlivening manner."

Janine Schmidt, MLib
University Librarian
University of Queensland, Australia

The Haworth Information Press
An Imprint of The Haworth Press, Inc.

Improved Access to Information: Portals, Content Selection, and Digital Information

Improved Access to Information: Portals, Content Selection, and Digital Information has been co-published simultaneously as *Journal of Library Administration*, Volume 39, Number 4 2003.

The *Journal of Library Administration* Monographic "Separates"

Below is a list of "separates," which in serials librarianship means a special issue simultaneously published as a special journal issue or double-issue *and* as a "separate" hardbound monograph. (This is a format which we also call a "DocuSerial.")

"Separates" are published because specialized libraries or professionals may wish to purchase a specific thematic issue by itself in a format which can be separately cataloged and shelved, as opposed to purchasing the journal on an on-going basis. Faculty members may also more easily consider a "separate" for classroom adoption.

"Separates" are carefully classified separately with the major book jobbers so that the journal tie-in can be noted on new book order slips to avoid duplicate purchasing.

You may wish to visit Haworth's Website at . . .

http://www.HaworthPress.com

. . . to search our online catalog for complete tables of contents of these separates and related publications.

You may also call 1-800-HAWORTH (outside US/Canada: 607-722-5857), or Fax 1-800-895-0582 (outside US/Canada: 607-771-0012), or e-mail at:

docdelivery@haworthpress.com

Improved Access to Information: Portals, Content Selection, and Digital Information, edited by Sul H. Lee (Vol. 39, No. 4, 2003). *Examines how improved electronic resources can allow libraries to provide an increasing amount of digital information to an ever-expanding patron base.*

Digital Images and Art Libraries in the Twenty-First Century, edited by Susan Wyngaard, MLS (Vol. 39, No. 2/3, 2003). *Provides an in-depth look at the technology that art librarians must understand in order to work effectively in today's digital environment.*

The Twenty-First Century Art Librarian, edited by Terrie L. Wilson, MLS (Vol. 39, No. 1, 2003). *"A MUST-READ addition to every art, architecture, museum, and visual resources library bookshelf." (Betty Jo Irvine, PhD, Fine Arts Librarian, Indiana University)*

The Strategic Stewardship of Cultural Resources: To Preserve and Protect, edited by Andrea T. Merrill, BA (Vol. 38, No. 1/2/3/4, 2003). *Leading library, museum, and archival professionals share their expertise on a wide variety of preservation and security issues.*

Distance Learning Library Services: The Tenth Off-Campus Library Services Conference, edited by Patrick B. Mahoney (Vol. 37, No. 1/2/3/4, 2002). *Explores the pitfalls of providing information services to distance students and suggests ways to avoid them.*

Electronic Resources and Collection Development, edited by Sul H. Lee (Vol. 36, No. 3, 2002). *Shows how electronic resources have impacted traditional collection development policies and practices.*

Information Literacy Programs: Successes and Challenges, edited by Patricia Durisin, MLIS (Vol. 36, No. 1/2, 2002). *Examines Web-based collaboration, teamwork with academic and administrative colleagues, evidence-based librarianship, and active learning strategies in library instruction programs.*

Evaluating the Twenty-First Century Library: The Association of Research Libraries New Measures Initiative, 1997-2001, edited by Donald L. DeWitt, PhD (Vol. 35, No. 4, 2001). *This collection of articles (thirteen of which previously appeared in ARL's bimonthly newsletter/ report on research issues and actions) examines the Association of Research Libraries' "new measures" initiative.*

Impact of Digital Technology on Library Collections and Resource Sharing, edited by Sul H. Lee (Vol. 35, No. 3, 2001). *Shows how digital resources have changed the traditional academic library.*

Libraries and Electronic Resources: New Partnerships, New Practices, New Perspectives, edited by Pamela L. Higgins (Vol. 35, No. 1/2, 2001). *An essential guide to the Internet's impact on electronic resources management past, present, and future.*

Diversity Now: People, Collections, and Services in Academic Libraries, edited by Teresa Y. Neely, PhD, and Kuang-Hwei (Janet) Lee-Smeltzer, MS, MSLIS (Vol. 33, No. 1/2/3/4, 2001). *Examines multicultural trends in academic libraries' staff and users, types of collections, and services offered.*

Leadership in the Library and Information Science Professions: Theory and Practice, edited by Mark D. Winston, MLS, PhD (Vol. 32, No. 3/4, 2001). *Offers fresh ideas for developing and using leadership skills, including recruiting potential leaders, staff training and development, issues of gender and ethnic diversity, and budget strategies for success.*

Off-Campus Library Services, edited by Ann Marie Casey (Vol. 31, No. 3/4, 2001 and Vol. 32, No. 1/2, 2001). *This informative volume examines various aspects of off-campus, or distance learning. It explores training issues for library staff, Web site development, changing roles for librarians, the uses of conferencing software, library support for Web-based courses, library agreements and how to successfully negotiate them, and much more!*

Research Collections and Digital Information, edited by Sul H. Lee (Vol. 31, No. 2, 2000). *Offers new strategies for collecting, organizing, and accessing library materials in the digital age.*

Academic Research on the Internet: Options for Scholars & Libraries, edited by Helen Laurence, MLS, EdD, and William Miller, MLS, PhD (Vol. 30, No. 1/2/3/4, 2000). *"Emphasizes quality over quantity. . . . Presents the reader with the best research-oriented Web sites in the field. A state-of-the-art review of academic use of the Internet as well as a guide to the best Internet sites and services. . . . A useful addition for any academic library." (David A. Tyckoson, MLS, Head of Reference, California State University, Fresno)*

Management for Research Libraries Cooperation, edited by Sul H. Lee (Vol. 29. No. 3/4, 2000). *Delivers sound advice, models, and strategies for increasing sharing between institutions to maximize the amount of printed and electronic research material you can make available in your library while keeping costs under control.*

Integration in the Library Organization, edited by Christine E. Thompson, PhD (Vol. 29, No. 2, 1999). *Provides librarians with the necessary tools to help libraries balance and integrate public and technical services and to improve the capability of libraries to offer patrons quality services and large amounts of information.*

Library Training for Staff and Customers, edited by Sara Ramser Beck, MLS, MBA (Vol. 29, No. 1, 1999). *This comprehensive book is designed to assist library professionals involved in presenting or planning training for library staff members and customers. You will explore ideas for effective general reference training, training on automated systems, training in specialized subjects such as African American history and biography, and training for areas such as patents and trademarks, and business subjects.* Library Training for Staff and Customers *answers numerous training questions and is an excellent guide for planning staff development.*

Collection Development in the Electronic Environment: Shifting Priorities, edited by Sul H. Lee (Vol. 28, No. 4, 1999). *Through case studies and firsthand experiences, this volume discusses meeting the needs of scholars at universities, budgeting issues, user education, staffing in the electronic age, collaborating libraries and resources, and how vendors meet the needs of different customers.*

The Age Demographics of Academic Librarians: A Profession Apart, by Stanley J. Wilder (Vol. 28, No. 3, 1999). *The average age of librarians has been increasing dramatically since 1990. This unique book will provide insights on how this demographic issue can impact a library and what can be done to make the effects positive.*

Collection Development in a Digital Environment, edited by Sul H. Lee (Vol. 28, No. 1, 1999). *Explores ethical and technological dilemmas of collection development and gives several suggestions on how a library can successfully deal with these challenges and provide patrons with the information they need.*

Scholarship, Research Libraries, and Global Publishing, by Jutta Reed-Scott (Vol. 27, No. 3/4, 1999). *This book documents a research project in conjunction with the Association of Research Libraries (ARL) that explores the issue of foreign acquisition and how it affects collection in international studies, area studies, collection development, and practices of international research libraries.*

Managing Multicultural Diversity in the Library: Principles and Issues for Administrators, edited by Mark Winston (Vol. 27, No. 1/2, 1999). *Defines diversity, clarifies why it is important to address issues of diversity, and identifies goals related to diversity and how to go about achieving those goals.*

Information Technology Planning, edited by Lori A. Goetsch (Vol. 26, No. 3/4, 1999). *Offers innovative approaches and strategies useful in your library and provides some food for thought about information technology as we approach the millennium.*

The Economics of Information in the Networked Environment, edited by Meredith A. Butler, MLS, and Bruce R. Kingma, PhD (Vol. 26, No. 1/2, 1998). *"A book that should be read both by information professionals and by administrators, faculty and others who share a collective concern to provide the most information to the greatest number at the lowest cost in the networked environment." (Thomas J. Galvin, PhD, Professor of Information Science and Policy, University at Albany, State University of New York)*

OCLC 1967-1997: Thirty Years of Furthering Access to the World's Information, edited by K. Wayne Smith (Vol. 25, No. 2/3/4, 1998). *"A rich–and poignantly personal, at times–historical account of what is surely one of this century's most important developments in librarianship." (Deanna B. Marcum, PhD, President, Council on Library and Information Resources, Washington, DC)*

Management of Library and Archival Security: From the Outside Looking In, edited by Robert K. O'Neill, PhD (Vol. 25, No. 1, 1998). *"Provides useful advice and on-target insights for professionals caring for valuable documents and artifacts." (Menzi L. Behrnd-Klodt, JD, Attorney/Archivist, Klodt and Associates, Madison, WI)*

Economics of Digital Information: Collection, Storage, and Delivery, edited by Sul H. Lee (Vol. 24, No. 4, 1997). *Highlights key concepts and issues vital to a library's successful venture into the digital environment and helps you understand why the transition from the printed page to the digital packet has been problematic for both creators of proprietary materials and users of those materials.*

The Academic Library Director: Reflections on a Position in Transition, edited by Frank D'Andraia, MLS (Vol. 24, No. 3, 1997). *"A useful collection to have whether you are seeking a position as director or conducting a search for one." (College & Research Libraries News)*

Emerging Patterns of Collection Development in Expanding Resource Sharing, Electronic Information, and Network Environment, edited by Sul H. Lee (Vol. 24, No. 1/2, 1997). *"The issues it deals with are common to us all. We all need to make our funds go further and our resources work harder, and there are ideas here which we can all develop." (The Library Association Record)*

Interlibrary Loan/Document Delivery and Customer Satisfaction: Strategies for Redesigning Services, edited by Pat L. Weaver-Meyers, Wilbur A. Stolt, and Yem S. Fong (Vol. 23, No. 1/2, 1997). *"No interlibrary loan department supervisor at any mid-sized to large college or university library can afford not to read this book." (Gregg Sapp, MLS, MEd, Head of Access Services, University of Miami, Richter Library, Coral Gables, Florida)*

Access, Resource Sharing and Collection Development, edited by Sul H. Lee (Vol. 22, No. 4, 1996). *Features continuing investigation and discussion of important library issues, specifically the role of libraries in acquiring, storing, and disseminating information in different formats.*

Managing Change in Academic Libraries, edited by Joseph J. Branin (Vol. 22, No. 2/3, 1996). *"Touches on several aspects of academic library management, emphasizing the changes that are occurring at the present time. . . . Recommended this title for individuals or libraries interested in management aspects of academic libraries." (RQ American Library Association)*

Libraries and Student Assistants: Critical Links, edited by William K. Black, MLS (Vol. 21, No. 3/4, 1995). *"A handy reference work on many important aspects of managing student assistants. . . . Solid, useful information on basic management issues in this work and several chapters are useful for experienced managers." (The Journal of Academic Librarianship)*

The Future of Resource Sharing, edited by Shirley K. Baker and Mary E. Jackson, MLS (Vol. 21, No. 1/2, 1995). *"Recommended for library and information science schools because of its balanced presentation of the ILL/document delivery issues." (Library Acquisitions: Practice and Theory)*

The Future of Information Services, edited by Virginia Steel, MA, and C. Brigid Welch, MLS (Vol. 20, No. 3/4, 1995). *"The leadership discussions will be useful for library managers as will the discussions of how library structures and services might work in the next century." (Australian Special Libraries)*

The Dynamic Library Organizations in a Changing Environment, edited by Joan Giesecke, MLS, DPA (Vol. 20, No. 2, 1995). *"Provides a significant look at potential changes in the library world and presents its readers with possible ways to address the negative results of such changes. . . . Covers the key issues facing today's libraries . . . Two thumbs up!" (Marketing Library Resources)*

Monographic "Separates" list continued at the back

Improved Access to Information: Portals, Content Selection, and Digital Information

Papers Presented at the 2003 University of Oklahoma Libraries Annual Conference

Sul H. Lee
Editor

Improved Access to Information: Portals, Content Selection, and Digital Information has been co-published simultaneously as *Journal of Library Administration*, Volume 39, Number 4 2003.

The Haworth Information Press®
An Imprint of The Haworth Press, Inc.

New York • London • Victoria (AU)
www.HaworthPress.com

Published by

The Haworth Information Press®, 10 Alice Street, Binghamton, NY 13904-1580 USA

The Haworth Information Press® is an imprint of The Haworth Press, Inc., 10 Alice Street, Binghamton, NY 13904-1580 USA.

Improved Access to Information: Portals, Content Selection, and Digital Information has been co-published simultaneously as *Journal of Library Administration*, Volume 39, Number 4 2003.

© 2003 by The Haworth Press, Inc. All rights reserved. No part of this work may be reproduced or utilized in any form or by any means, electronic or mechanical, including photocopying, microfilm and recording, or by any information storage and retrieval system, without permission in writing from the publisher. Printed in the United States of America.

The development, preparation, and publication of this work has been undertaken with great care. However, the publisher, employees, editors, and agents of The Haworth Press and all imprints of The Haworth Press, Inc., including The Haworth Medical Press® and Pharmaceutical Products Press®, are not responsible for any errors contained herein or for consequences that may ensue from use of materials or information contained in this work. Opinions expressed by the author(s) are not necessarily those of The Haworth Press, Inc. With regard to case studies, identities and circumstances of individuals discussed herein have been changed to protect confidentiality. Any resemblance to actual persons, living or dead, is entirely coincidental.

Cover design by Brooke R. Stiles.

Library of Congress Cataloging-in-Publication Data

University of Oklahoma. Libraries. Conference (2003)
Improved access to information : portals, content selection, and digital information / Sul H. Lee, editor.
    p. cm.
    Papers presented at the 2003 University of Oklahoma Libraries Annual Conference.
    "Co-published simultaneously as Journal of library administration, Volume 39, Number 4, 2003."
    Includes bibliographical references and index.
    ISBN 0-7890-2444-6 (alk. paper) – ISBN 0-7890-2445-4 (pbk. : alk. paper)
    1. Libraries–Special collections–Electronic information resources–Congresses. 2. Libraries–United States–Special collections–Electronic information resources–Congresses. 3. Digital libraries–Collection development–Congresses. 4. Academic libraries–Collection development–Congresses. 5. Research libraries–Collection development–Congresses. 6. Library Web sites– Congresses. 7. Web portals–Congresses. I. Lee, Sul H. II. Journal of library administration. III. Title.
Z692.C65U54 2003
025'.00285–dc22

2003027496

Indexing, Abstracting & Website/Internet Coverage

This section provides you with a list of major indexing & abstracting services. That is to say, each service began covering this periodical during the year noted in the right column. Most Websites which are listed below have indicated that they will either post, disseminate, compile, archive, cite or alert their own Website users with research-based content from this work. (This list is as current as the copyright date of this publication.)

Abstracting, Website/Indexing Coverage . . . . Year When Coverage Began

- *Academic Abstracts/CD-ROM* 1993
- *Academic Search: database of 2,000 selected academic serials,*
    updated monthly: EBSCO Publishing 1995
- *Academic Search Elite (EBSCO)* 1993
- *AGRICOLA Database <http://www.natl.usda.gov/ag98>* 1991
- *Business & Company ProFile ASAP on CD-ROM*
    <http://www.galegroup.com> 1996
- *Business ASAP* 1993
- *Business ASAP–International <http://www.galegroup.com>* 1984
- *Business International and Company ProFile ASAP*
    <http://www.galegroup.com> 1996
- *CNPIEC Reference Guide: Chinese National Directory*
    of Foreign Periodicals 1995
- *Current Articles on Library Literature and Services (CALLS)* 1992
- *Current Cites [Digital Libraries] [Electronic Publishing] [Multimedia &*
    Hypermedia] [Networks & Networking] [General] 2000
- *Current Index to Journals in Education* 1986
- *Educational Administration Abstracts (EAA)* 1991
- *Environmental Sciences and Pollution Management (Cambridge Scientific*
    Abstracts Internet Database Service) <http://www.csa.com> . . . . *
- *FRANCIS. INIST/CNRS <http://www.inist.fr>* 1986
- *General BusinessFile ASAP <http://www.galegroup.com>* 1993
- *General BusinessFile ASAP–International <http://galegroup.com>* 1984

(continued)

(continued)

*Exact start date to come.

Special Bibliographic Notes related to special journal issues
(separates) and indexing/abstracting:

- indexing/abstracting services in this list will also cover material in any "separate" that is co-published simultaneously with Haworth's special thematic journal issue or DocuSerial. Indexing/abstracting usually covers material at the article/chapter level.
- monographic co-editions are intended for either non-subscribers or libraries which intend to purchase a second copy for their circulating collections.
- monographic co-editions are reported to all jobbers/wholesalers/approval plans. The source journal is listed as the "series" to assist the prevention of duplicate purchasing in the same manner utilized for books-in-series.
- to facilitate user/access services all indexing/abstracting services are encouraged to utilize the co-indexing entry note indicated at the bottom of the first page of each article/chapter/contribution.
- this is intended to assist a library user of any reference tool (whether print, electronic, online, or CD-ROM) to locate the monographic version if the library has purchased this version but not a subscription to the source journal.
- individual articles/chapters in any Haworth publication are also available through the Haworth Document Delivery Service (HDDS).

For Melissa

Improved Access to Information: Portals, Content Selection, and Digital Information

CONTENTS

ABOUT THE EDITOR

Sul H. Lee, Dean of the University Libraries at the University of Oklahoma, is an internationally recognized leader and consultant in the library administration and management field. Dean Lee is a past member of the Board of Directors, Association of Research Libraries, the ARL Office of Management Services Advisory Committee, and the Council for the American Library Association. His works include *The Impact of Rising Costs of Serials and Monographs on Library Services and Programs*; *Library Material Costs and Access to Information*; *Budgets for Acquisitions: Strategies for Serials, Monographs, and Electronic Formats*; *Vendor Evaluation and Acquisition Budgets*; *The Role and Future of Special Collections in Research Libraries*; *Declining Acquisitions Budgets*; *Access, Ownership, and Resource Sharing*; and *Electronic Resources and Collection Development*. He is Editor of the *Journal of Library Administration*.

∞ ALL HAWORTH INFORMATION PRESS
BOOKS AND JOURNALS ARE PRINTED
ON CERTIFIED ACID-FREE PAPER

Introduction

Sul H. Lee

Most librarians would agree that the academic library community has accepted the concept of the digital library and acknowledged the value and utility of electronic information. Students and scholars, also, have embraced enthusiastically the availability of digital resources in the academic library. The question for contemporary librarians is no longer one of moving into the digital information arena, but how to improve access to the electronic resources now available to library users.

The 2003 University of Oklahoma Libraries annual conference focused on the challenge of improving access to digital information via portals and content selection. Nine internationally known librarians addressed these issues and gave conference attendees their views on how research libraries were meeting the challenge of improved access to electronic information.

James Michalko, president of Research Libraries Group, Inc., gave the opening address and posed the interesting question "For whom is the library an anchor?" He noted that research libraries produce portals with the expectation of creating anchor sites that will provide essential services to their users and secure their user base. His paper outlines the library community's understanding of user needs, how researcher use of electronic information is evolving, and how libraries are responding to their changing roles.

University of Washington Libraries director, Lizabeth A. Wilson, explores how libraries are using what is known about user preferences and search behaviors to create access points. She concludes that libraries responding to the needs of students and faculty will be successful in building solid and loyal user bases.

While access to digital information is rapidly becoming a major challenge

[Haworth co-indexing entry note]: "Introduction." Lee, Sul H. Co-published simultaneously in *Journal of Library Administration* (The Haworth Information Press, an imprint of The Haworth Press, Inc.) Vol. 39, No. 4, 2003, pp. 1-3; and: *Improved Access to Information: Portals, Content Selection, and Digital Information* (ed: Sul H. Lee) The Haworth Information Press, an imprint of The Haworth Press, Inc., 2003, pp. 1-3. Single or multiple copies of this article are available for a fee from The Haworth Document Delivery Service [1-800-HAWORTH, 9:00 a.m. - 5:00 p.m. (EST). E-mail address: docdelivery@haworthpress.com].

http://www.haworthpress.com/web/JLA
© 2003 by The Haworth Press, Inc. All rights reserved.
Digital Object Identifier: 10.1300/J111v39n04_01

1

for collection management librarians, Bernard F. Reilly, president of The Center for Research Libraries, correctly observes that print collections continue to grow unabated. He also suggests in his paper that research libraries have made substantial progress toward a cooperative management of print research collections.

Joseph J. Branin, director of Libraries at Ohio State University, notes that digital age librarians have made a professional distinction between collection development and collection management and they now are moving one step further to knowledge management. In his article, he outlines the history of these changes, defines knowledge management, and provides some examples of how the Ohio State University Libraries has changed in response to this shift.

The Association of Research Libraries (ARL) has always been on the cutting edge of new developments in librarianship and it is not surprising that two of ARL's recent initiatives support the implementation of portals in research libraries. Mary E. Jackson, senior program officer for access services at the Association of Research Libraries, provides an overview of the scope and progress of these initiatives.

How digital collections are developed is the topic of Edward Shreeves, associate director of the University of Iowa Libraries. His paper examines the role of the selector as he compares traditional collection development criteria to the acquisition of aggregate packages of electronic resources that are so much a part of today's collection development programs.

Alice Prochaska, university librarian for Yale University, draws upon her past experience at the British Library and her current position as head of a research library with strong special collections, to comment on making local special collections available globally. She discusses the ethics of sharing and the setting of priorities for making unique local research collections available to worldwide audiences.

Barbara I. Dewey, dean of libraries at the University of Tennessee, has noted that how a library makes portals available is as important to researchers as is access to the information gained from their use. Her paper, "Portals and the Human Factor: Bringing Virtual Services to the Life of the Mind or the Scholarly Stargate," discusses supporting services for portals and portals that have been developed without a model.

The Online Computer Library Center (OCLC) is a worldwide leader in developing models for electronic access to information, and Lorcan Dempsey, OCLC's vice president for research, uses an analogy from genetic research to describe the unfolding of new environments that will lead researchers to the information sources they seek. His paper, "The Recombinant Library: Portals and People," offers examples of how this process may benefit those using research libraries.

Together, the combined presentations from the 2003 University of Oklahoma Libraries conference provide an overview of the thoughts of the nation's leading librarians and information service executives on improving access to information. The ideas they present have relevance to all libraries as they continue to develop their electronic resources. The papers will also serve as milestones for future library historians as they write about the development of electronic resources in the 21st century. We are pleased to make these ideas and solutions available to a wider audience by publishing them in both journal and monograph formats.

For Whom Is the Library an Anchor?
Observations on Library Portals

James Michalko

OPENING WELCOME

I'm pleased to be here with you and to start our conference where we will reflect on and discuss improved access to information: portals, content selection and digital information. I realize that, across the range of the presentations, we'll be looking at each of these elements separately as well as together. My pleasant task at the beginning of our time together is to provide some observations on library portals–the service manifestation of our desire to improve access to information as well as the library's primary mode for disseminating digital information. I thought it might be useful to get us started by providing some context, some observations, some stipulations that might underpin our discussion and be useful throughout the conference. Then I'll focus on library portals themselves–what are they? where are we in the development life-cycle of these mechanisms? what are the challenges to their realization? what is going to make library portals an anchor for the audiences you serve? what are the tools and the services that will make the library portal a primary destination? and finally I'll say a few things about where we should be looking for guidance on tools and services.

Let me turn to the context I mentioned, those fixed points that might serve to underpin our discussions of portals, content selection and digital information. I've got seven stipulations that I'd like to put forward.

James Michalko is President, Research Libraries Group, Inc., Mountain View, CA.

[Haworth co-indexing entry note]: "For Whom Is the Library an Anchor? Observations on Library Portals." Michalko, James. Co-published simultaneously in *Journal of Library Administration* (The Haworth Information Press, an imprint of The Haworth Press, Inc.) Vol. 39, No. 4, 2003, pp. 5-17; and: *Improved Access to Information: Portals, Content Selection, and Digital Information* (ed: Sul H. Lee) The Haworth Information Press, an imprint of The Haworth Press, Inc., 2003, pp. 5-17. Single or multiple copies of this article are available for a fee from The Haworth Document Delivery Service [1-800-HAWORTH, 9:00 a.m. - 5:00 p.m. (EST). E-mail address: docdelivery@haworthpress.com].

http://www.haworthpress.com/web/JLA
© 2003 by The Haworth Press, Inc. All rights reserved.
Digital Object Identifier: 10.1300/J111v39n04_02

THE CONTEXT AND SOME STIPULATIONS

The Shift to Electronic Resources Has Happened

The shift is reflected both in library spending patterns as well as the preference and use patterns of our constituencies. Certainly the library community has been aware of this for quite awhile. For the broader higher education community it may have become most widely understood when *The Chronicle of Higher Education* published its article on "The Deserted Library" and appended a graphic showing that spending on electronic resources at one SUNY campus had gone up six times over the previous decade reaching nearly a third of its materials spending in 2001.[1] They didn't pick an outlier for this observation; the ARL statistics have been showing this shift for quite some time. As ARL said when they released the most recent 2001 numbers, "After almost a decade of data collection, certain trends have become clear. The average percentage of the library budget that is spent on electronic materials was 16.25% in 2000-01, nearly five times as much as in 1992-93. Almost $132 million was reported spent on electronic resources in 2000-01, by 106 universities. The vast majority of these expenditures increases have gone towards the purchase of electronic serials and subscription services. Whereas only $11 million was reported spent in this area when it was first included on the survey in 1994-95, 106 libraries reported electronic serials expenditures totaling more than $117 million today."[2]

Students Misperceive the Electronic Domain as a Complete Environment

As one university survey put it, "Another problem is that with more electronic resources, user expectations increase. If they can get some of our collection electronically, they want to get all of our collection electronically. Worse, they often avoid resources that aren't easily accessible. A math professor admitted to us that he only reads journals that we subscribe to electronically. This aversion to print is seen in the citation lists of student papers. Citation lists are dominated by articles that are easily accessible. As students have become accustomed to working electronically we have found them citing fewer print-only resources."[3] And that is a shame but it is also an accurate description of the current state of affairs. One that we all know echoes previous episodes in the transformation of library services. All we need recall is the mixed environment when the automated library catalog was being introduced alongside the card catalog. Many of the same misperceptions prevailed then. It is a misperception that we can work to overcome but it is a perception with which we will simply have to work.

Good scholarship, good teaching, good learning are the products of hard work. I was struck by the observation in an article about the ascendancy of Google that in a sidelong way made the same point. "It's the collapse of inconvenience," says Siva Vaidhyanathan, assistant professor of culture and communication at New York University. "It turns out that inconvenience was a really important part of our lives, and we didn't realize it."[4] Inconvenience–hard work–is an important ingredient in creating something worthwhile.

[As a side comment: I'd urge you to watch for the forthcoming book, intriguingly titled *The Anarchist in the Library* by Vaidhyanathan; editorial reviews suggest it's an interesting study of the impacts of peer-to-peer networking on a whole variety of social and cultural conventions.]

Limits on What the Library Can Do About This State of Affairs

In this regard, I find the observation by Nicholas Burckel, the library dean at Marquette University, fairly compelling. He argued that increasing use of the libraries' traditional materials relies on good pedagogical strategies in the classroom more than on what the library can do on its own. "If you allow a student in your course to get an A, and he or she has not consulted primary sources, and you have not required them to use print sources, there's no way the library can make that happen."[5]

Nostalgia for Formerly Normative Behavior Is Understandable But Unproductive

To a certain extent the current patterns of electronic materials use may be anti-intellectual, they may be engendering a fast-food mentality of scholarship, and it may be that the quality of the information that some students use has been degraded, but as an important part of the support structure in higher education, libraries cannot afford to imagine that we are in a position to rewind the paradigm. While we lament information illiteracy and urge more education and provide more training, the users have a different opinion. They think of themselves as adept and skillful at using online information even though they may have little or no formal instruction in information gathering.[6] Our job is to understand these expectations and patterns and deliver the quality, the trusted, the authoritative, and the important within the newly established paradigm.

Renewed Emphasis on the Library as Social Environment Is Not Entirely a Bad Thing

If our students are not coming to the library for traditional materials the phenomenon perhaps represents a different kind of opportunity for the library to assert one of its contributions to campus life–the physical place as a social environment. I know that there continues to be great divergence in the perception and experiences of libraries about whether this is true, in whether students are, in fact, not coming to the library, as measured in circulation statistics and turnstile counts. Nevertheless there are a variety of surveys that indicate loss of users no matter how measured. We've always known that libraries in a campus environment were about more than the materials but the electronic challenge of the Web has perhaps highlighted once again this other important role of the library even while we struggle to find new modes of providing the materials of education and research. The library will be an important physical place as long as university members desire and value community.

We Have Learned a Number of Things About Users, the Internet, and the Electronic Environment

The recent Outsell survey of the "Dimensions and Use of the Scholarly Information Environment" sponsored by the Digital Library Federation and The Council on Library and Information Resources[7] is the dominant touchstone for what we've learned. We're still extracting all of its meaning but the basic lessons affirmed what we've seen on our campuses or confirmed the local institutional studies that are now emerging on the landscape. The principal take-away from the survey is that "despite the triumph of print as a reliable source of information, most of the respondents tended to go first to online sources in studies and research. Almost 90 percent of researchers said they went online first, then consulted print sources. About 75 percent of students said they used the Internet first, then went to a professor or librarian for assistance and consulted print sources last."[8]

We Know that Not All Libraries Are the Same

I think we should stipulate to this right at the beginning of our conference. Even in our homogeneity we are different. Our clients and their needs differ in a variety of local ways, our resources differ, our histories differ and our experiences and circumstances differ even while we may share a common, high-level commitment to improved access to information. Anything said over the course of the conference will have at least one counter-example.

PORTALS DEFINED

Having set this context and with those stipulations as background, let me turn to a discussion of portals and the particular ways that library portals are being approached. During this conference we're likely to use this word in a variety of ways including some that are metaphoric–"the library itself is a portal to knowledge." I'm sure the metaphors and analogies will be illuminating but I want to talk more specifically about web portals. The word has been used in a variety of ways and what it denotes is still evolving. In general, however, the word has been used to characterize web sites commonly known for searching and navigation tools. Around 1996, a portal was the place where available content from the Internet was cataloged, acting as a hub from which users could locate and link to desired content.[9]

Michael Looney and Peter Lyman define the web portal as "systems which gather a variety of useful information resources into a single 'one stop' web page, helping the user to avoid being overwhelmed by 'infoglut' or feeling lost on the Web."[10]

The CIC Library Survey on Portals started with an interesting and useful definition which got expanded by the survey participants. I think it is apt for this conference. "A portal, as compared to a web site, gateway or structure, leads a user to a set of information AND enables that user to personalize his/her page–to select and include chosen links on that personal page–AND is sensitive to a person's role within the institution (even before the user has personalized it)."[11] The emphasis on personalization and role here I think is important. It is what makes it possible to think about a *library* portal as distinct from just a collection of links and bookmarks. A library portal assumes that the users have a particular role in the academic enterprise and assumes that they are seeking information in support of teaching, study or research. Those assumptions inform the kinds of content that will be presented and the types of associated tools and services that will be provided, making the site into a library portal.

LIBRARY PORTALS

Right now there is certainly a lot of energy and activity in the academic library community going into realizing some version of a library portal. More energy is expended in discussions of definition and desirability than into actual portal building but the early innovators and builders in the university community have done some very interesting and valuable work. A universe of examples is emerging, some better than others, but the points of reference are out there: MyLibrary@NCState, My Gateway from the Libraries at the University of Washington, and many others. One way to think about these efforts, and library portals more generally, is as updated embodiments of the ways in which the library delivers on its academic mission. As one library director puts it, "The library's mission in the old days was to acquire, organize and make information available. It's being rearticulated now as a pointer, an entity that provides a way to link users and knowledge together–to be a portal, an organized entrée to information. And it's not just physical. It's also virtual."[12]

Building a library portal may be one of the ways to deliver on the library's mission but why is this kind of effort capturing so much of our attention, energy and resources now? Why are we doing this? One response in a paper I reviewed recently gives this rationale: "Academic libraries exist for the purpose of collecting, organizing and disseminating information. They help students become lifelong learners and enable faculty and students to maintain superior research activities. Libraries have to maximize their visibility and usefulness especially to our primary customers–our own students and faculty. *In short, branding is important for libraries* [my emphasis].The development of personalized and customizable web portals or gateways is an important tool for enabling our customers' better access to the information they need."[13] ". . . In order to survive and stay relevant in this information environment, libraries have to create environments and services that respond to user needs directly, interactively and in a timely fashion."[14]

As the previous observation indicates, what's driving library portal development is partly fear of disintermediation; the library will lose its role and its brand. And there are good reasons why we should be afraid of such a scenario. But more importantly I think the momentum comes from a devotion to our service mission and new set of slowly emerging understandings of what our users expect and want. We're realizing that what our users want are the traits that characterize the best of the Web–the experiences provided by Google, Yahoo, and Amazon.com. Library portals that can deliver similar traits are one way for libraries to effectively manifest our mission to our current, albeit drifting, academic clientele.

While we forge ahead in our investigation, our construction and our operation of library portals, I think it's good to remember a few things about the current efforts.

LIBRARY PORTALS ARE NOT UBIQUITOUS

It's important to note that this approach, for all its potential merits, still represents a minority approach. As reported in April 2002, only six of the 77 responding ARL libraries had a library portal.[15] Many more had intentions and activities underway which may now have been realized but it's still far too early to consider library portals as an accepted, expected and universal library response.

LIBRARY PORTALS ARE IN THEIR INFANCY

In addition to the levels of commitment evidenced by the small numbers, I suggest that the low level of functionality, constrained content coverage, modest tool provision, and restricted service array are strong indications that, as a community, we are only just now starting to imagine what a mature library portal could actually deliver. As a reminder, the ARL survey I cited set a very basic hurdle when they defined a library portal as including "(1) search engine tools that offer the user the capability to search across multiple sources and integrate the results of those searches, and (2) at least one kind of supporting service for the user (such as requesting retrieval or delivery of non-digital material, online reference help, etc.)."[16] This is a pretty low hurdle. To imagine that something as basic as this portal could grow into the personalized, customizable destination that I defined earlier is possible, but not obvious.

LIBRARY PORTALS FACE SOME SIGNIFICANT OBSTACLES TO SUCCESS

Before a library even encounters the intrinsic challenges of content, tools and services, there are external obstacles to successful implementations. The role of the library portal relative to the university's portal is a dilemma, and sorting this out can be a very large challenge in the realization of a library portal. In many cases library portal work is waiting on university-wide decisions about the nature and form of the university portal to be announced. And as we know, university commitments to portals are both difficult to make and equally difficult to sustain. As Richard Katz of EDUCAUSE has said, "A portal strategy is difficult and perilous because so many on campus are weary and suspicious of yet another new enterprise-wide information technology initiative, and because portal initiatives, by definition, require across-the-institution agreements on approach and design that are hard to achieve in loosely coupled organizations like academic institutions."[17] Even when the prerequisite commitment to a portal strategy is in place at an institution, that does not mean that the effort will succeed as the University of Michigan's withdrawal from its portal project concretely demonstrates. In that instance the university administrator responsible for the project announced that he was "skeptical of attempts within a single university to build something and sustain it internally over the long haul," speculating that while they are still interested in what a portal can do for the community they are not interested in going it alone and feel strongly that open-source software in some sort of collaborative effort might be more promising.[18] If you sort the library and university roles satisfactorily and make the necessary commitments to a strategy, you may still encounter a showstopping obstacle; one that was singled out earlier at one of these conferences–the necessary university infrastructure is missing. When Paula Kaufman rightly made that observation she specifically mentioned the lack of standards and protocols for authentication and authorization.[19] It still applies. In sum, I think the perils of across-the-institution efforts, the difficulty of solo construction and the significant gaps in the infrastructure are the underlying reasons that there are so few library portals right now and that their desired characteristics still remain undefined.

Given these systemic obstacles I think it's still too early to tell whether a library portal is going to be the necessary or preferred vehicle in which libraries manifest their service mission to their constituents. At this stage in development, the trend could yet turn out to have the trajectory of the Campus-Wide Information Systems of twenty years ago where the degrees of difficulty associated with their construction hindered them so much that they were overtaken by another information delivery mechanism external to the institution–the World Wide Web. We could still have a similar external phenomenon overtake the library portal movement. In addition to the obvious commercial encroachment you might want to watch the kinds of services that get developed by the scholarly and disciplinary societies. On a number of dimensions they have some significant advantages as potential destination sites that could compete with or complement the library's portal efforts.

WHAT IS GOING TO MAKE LIBRARY PORTALS AN ANCHOR FOR THE AUDIENCES YOU SERVE?

Despite all of this, I think the construction of library portals is going to press forward–momentum and expectations are building. We still have time, however, to wrestle with the question of what will make these portals anchor sites for the audiences served by the library. When I say anchor site I don't mean that library portals will be the first destination for these audiences, but that they will be one of the preferred, primary destinations for these audiences.

I think the library has some advantages going for it in achieving that goal. The first advantage is content. You have the power to purchase and present what these audiences want. What you present will manifest the hybrid library of physical materials, electronic materials both leased and locally created, as well as the external information sources to which you link. This combination is coming together and we're working through some of the inherent problems in creating the hybrid library. As it emerges it will be a powerful resource for our audience. We have things they need.

The second advantage is that libraries are trusted. In a Columbia University study many of the students reported that they only use sites that are linked to the school, with the assumption that this means the site or database is "approved."[20]

The Outsell respondents said that they use the Internet and rely on it heavily. However, they trust the library more. Fifty-five percent report that they verify the accuracy of Internet resources. I found it amusing that the Cal Poly library portal actually features links to parody sites as a way to demonstrate the unreliability of much web information. This trust in the library and in print sources, combined with the overwhelming initial reliance on online sources, is a compelling disconnect.[21] It calls the question of how can libraries leverage this unique ability to deliver content while taking advantage of the well-earned trust that audiences place in them? Can you leverage it to make the movement towards library portals a success? To make your library portal a success for your audiences?

I think you can and I think the way you leverage content and trust is with tools and services. It's the presence of compelling tools and services that will bring your audience to these sites. As I recall overhearing at a conference some years ago, "Content that you can interact with in ways of your own choosing is no longer culture, it's a service." Of course, the ways that you can interact with content depend very much on the kinds of tools and services supporting that interaction.

WHAT ARE THE TOOLS AND THE SERVICES THAT WILL MAKE THE LIBRARY PORTAL A PRIMARY DESTINATION?

I don't know all of them but personalization (letting me customize my experience), recommendation (sensible, relevant suggestions and relationships) and introduction capabilities (brokering connections between me and the people with whom I might want to interact) are highly valued in other online venues, and I expect these are the traits of the successful Internet sites to which our audience is drawn and where their expectations have been fixed. We ought to be sure that our portals reflect those traits. To date, the personalization features of library portals are rudimentary; the recommendation and introduction functions are essentially non-existent. I think those will have to be reflected in future, mature library portals if we're to really satisfy our student audience. For a thought-provoking journey in this regard you should try visiting the 20 large web sites where the proportion of traffic from college students is particularly high. I think you'll be struck by all the ways in which personalization, recommendation and introducer capabilities have been honed *and* the depth of their absence from library portals.[22]

Having said that, I know, as you do, that any tools and services we provide are going to vary according to the segment of the academic audience you are trying to reach. We are all well aware of the undergraduate, graduate, faculty distinctions as well as those imparted by disciplinary differences. You can already see these audience distinctions reflected in the library portal service arrays and tool kits deployed by our early innovative institutions. Undergraduates get class help and course evaluations at the UofW, while graduate students get dissertation management tools at Virginia Commonwealth, and faculty get support for building and populating course web pages at Cal Poly. As these kinds of role distinctions in the audience get acknowledged in the library portal we're going to have to address even more complexity. Think of the difficulties and challenges that must be overcome in order to tailor these services for the distinctions engendered by age, stage of study or career. That degree of difficulty is only going to get accentuated if you look a bit behind our current audience and see what is coming from the generation about to enter university study. There's going to be another huge shift, perhaps more in degree than kind, and it is about to arrive on our doorstep. Addressing this complexity is daunting but essential if libraries intend to reach and serve their audiences effectively.

WHERE SHOULD WE BE LOOKING FOR GUIDANCE ON TOOLS AND SERVICES?

I have two suggestions. We should be looking more often towards the commercial sector and we should be watching the research on our future users (teenagers).

There's a major lesson from the commercial sector that we need to learn and it has to do with saving people time. Here's where we might find the common ground between our service mission and the way the commercial sector values tools and services. Commercial users have some similar characteristics to their knowledge worker counterparts in industry. And the most important is that they are running out of time. In the commercial sector, content users spend upwards of 16 percent of their time obtaining, reviewing and analyzing external information. One can sensibly imagine that, given the nature of education and teaching, students and faculty of all types spend much more of their workweek on similar tasks. The commercial sector has estimated the value of these information access costs–a recent study puts it at $10,000 per year per professional employee. Now granted, universities are not well positioned nor inclined to try and estimate student and faculty time in the same way, but the opportunity costs of information thrashing in the academic sector certainly cannot be much smaller.[23]

The issue here is to really understand the processes and practices in which our users engage. We have to design the library portal capabilities to mirror and support those information-seeking habits that have already been formed. And it is not just the information-seeking processes that need to be modeled; we need to create environments that mirror the multi-tasking characteristics of the borderless social and work "convenience" mix that students expect. Students use the most convenient computer, the one "at hand" to go on the Internet, they don't distinguish between work and social activity online, they don't distinguish between work, home and leisure. They open and use multiple applications simultaneously. They've got instant messaging going, e-mail, web browsing, word processing, etc., all going on at once.[24] That's the environment into which our portals have to fit. If our library portals can provide applications that save time and do it within the context of that "convenience" environment, we'll deliver something important and valued to our desired audience and we'll regain some of the lost users.

The other set of behavior and need patterns that should inform our thinking about tools and services are those evidenced by our future users–the teenage population. College students rely on information-seeking habits formed prior to arriving at college. One recent study found that 94% of online teens have used the Internet for school research and 71% used it as the major source for a recent school project.[25] The Pew Internet and American Life Project released a report on the school-related uses of the Internet by 11-19 year-olds called *The Digital Disconnect: The Widening Gap Between Internet-Savvy Students and Their Schools.* I think their key findings read like a tools and services wish list. They say students in this age group, those who are just about to become our audience, regard the Internet as

- a virtual textbook and reference library,
- a virtual tutor and study shortcut,
- a virtual study group,
- a virtual guidance counselor, and as a
- virtual locker, backpack and notebook.[26]

These findings don't tell you exactly what applications you ought to build into the library portal but they give you a very good sense of what is valued. They raise a variety of questions about where in this roster of desired deliverables the library wants to position itself, about what kind of surrounding and supporting capabilities the library portal must have, and how far beyond our traditional service offerings we might have to go if we want the library brand to be front and center in the online lives of our coming audience.

CLOSING

While I've talked a lot about the complex challenges associated with the library portal movement I'd like to signal my enthusiasm for the efforts and what the library community will learn. Struggle towards this service goal is worthwhile regardless of whether the library portal becomes a common and required element. What is really heartening is that the movement has engendered a new alertness to our users, focused our study of what they want, and created an operating frame in which the opportunities for integration of digital information into the library service portfolio are much more evident.

NOTES

1. Scott Carlson, "The Deserted Library," *The Chronicle of Higher Education*, 16 November 2001, <http://chronicle.com/free/v48/i12/12a03501.htm> (27 February 2003).

2. Mark Young, Martha Kyrillidou, and Julia Blixrud, "ARL Supplementary Statistics 2000-01," press release, *ARL Webpage*, 7 July 2002, <http://www.arl.org/stats/announce/sup01pr.html> (27 February 2003).

3. Sue Roppel, "Simon Fraser University Library Faculty Survey Results," *Simon Fraser University Webpage*, 7 June 2001, <http://www.lib.sfu.ca/about/reports/survey2001/faculty_report.pdf> (27 February 2003).

4. Neil Swidey, "A Nation of Voyeurs," *The Boston Globe Magazine*, 2 February 2003, <http://www.boston.com/globe/magazine/2003/0202/coverstory_entire.htm> (27 February 2003).

5. Scott Carlson, "Do Libraries Really Need Books," *The Chronicle of Higher Education*, 12 July 2002, <http://chronicle.com/free/v48/i44/44a03101.htm> (27 February 2003).

6. Lynn Dagar and Leigh Watson Healy, "TrendAlert: What The Dot.Com Survivors Can Teach Us," *Outsell Information*[SM] *Briefing, Outsell 60 Company Monitor*[SM] vol. 2, no. 1, 17 January 2003.

7. Amy Friedlander, *Dimensions and Use of the Scholarly Information Environment: Introduction to a Data Set Assembled by the Digital Library Federation and Outsell, Inc.*, (Washington, DC: Digital Library Federation Council on Library and Information Resources, 2002).

8. Scott Carlson, "Students and Faculty Turn to Online Library Materials Before Printed Ones, Study Finds," *The Chronicle of Higher Education*, 3 October 2003, <http://chronicle.com/free/2002/10/2002100301t.htm> (27 February 2003).

9. Debra Rundle, *Princeton University Homepage*, December 1999, <http://www.princeton.edu/~rundle/PrincetonPortal.htm> (27 February 2003).

10. Rundle, *op. cit.*

11. Committee on Institutional Cooperation (CIC) Library Survey on Portals, November 2001, <http://www.cic.uiuc.edu/groups/LibraryInfoTechDirectors/archive/Report/CICLibrarySurveyonPortals.pdf> (27 February 2003).

12. Carslon, *op. cit.*

13. Amos Lakos, "Personalized Library Portals and Organisational Change," *Proceedings of the 7th International Conference of European University Information Systems,* Berlin Humboldt-University, March, 2001 (EUNIS 2001).<http://edoc.hu-berlin.de/abstract.php3?id=3000600&lang=eng> (27 February 2003).

14. Lakos, *op. cit.*

15. Association of Research Libraries (ARL), "Portal Functionality Provided by ARL Libraries: Preliminary Results of an ARL Survey, April 11, 2002," *ARL Webpage,* <http://www.arl.org/access/scholarsportal/prelim.html#fn> (27 February 2003).

16. ARL, *op. cit.*

17. Richard N. Katz, "It's a Bird. It's a Plane. It's a Portal?" *EDUCAUSE Quarterly,* 38:3 (2000), 10-11. <http://www.educause.edu/ir/library/pdf/eq/a003/eqm0038.pdf> (27 February 2003).

18. Florence Olsen, "U. of Michigan Cancels a Closely Watched Portal Project," *The Chronicle of Higher Education,* 11 April 2002. <http://chronicle.com/free/2002/04/2002041101t.htm> (27 February 2003).

19. Paula Kaufman, "Whose Good Old Days Are These? A Dozen Predictions for the Digital Age," *Journal of Library Administration,* vol. 35, no. 3, 2001, 5-19.

20. "The Use of Electronic Resources Among Undergraduate and Graduate Students: Summary of Key Findings for Student Interviews," Electronic Publishing Initiative at Columbia (EPIC), September 2001. <http://www.epic.columbia.edu/eval/find03.html> (27 February 2003).

21. Carlson, *op. cit.*

22. Lee Rainie, Max Kalehoff and Dan Hess, "College Students and the Web," *Pew Internet & American Life Project Data Memo,* September 2002.<http://www.pewinternet.org/reports/toc.asp?Report=73> (27 February 2003)–data attributable to *comScore Media Metrix,* August 2002, a division of comScore Networks. <http://www.comscore.com/>.

23. Dagar and Healy, *op. cit.*

24. Steve Jones, principal, "The Internet Goes to College: How Students Are Living in the Future with Today's Technology," *Pew Internet & American Life Project,* 15 September 2002. <http://www.pewinternet.org/reports/toc.asp?Report=71> (27 February 2003).

25. Amanda Lenhart, Maya Simon, Mike Graziano, principals, "The Internet and Education: Findings of the Pew Internet & American Life Project," *Pew Internet & American Life Project,* 1 September 2001. <http://www.pewinternet.org/reports/toc.asp?Report=39> (27 February 2003).

26. Douglas Levin and Sousan Arafeh, "The Digital Disconnect: The Widening Gap Between Internet-Savvy Students and Their Schools," *Pew Internet & American Life Project,* 14 August 2002. <http://www.pewinternet.org/reports/toc.asp?Report=67> (27 February 2003).

If We Build It, Will They Come? Library Users in a Digital World

Lizabeth A. Wilson

Being born and raised in Iowa, and a baseball fan to boot, it should be no surprise that one of my favorite movies is *Field of Dreams*. For those not familiar with the film, let me set the scene.

Ray Kinsella, an Iowa farmer, is standing in the middle of a cornfield when he hears the voice for the first time. "If you build it, they will come." He looks around and doesn't see anybody. The voice speaks again, soft and confidential. "If you build it, they will come." Ray hears other cryptic messages, such as "Go the distance."

With an idealistic and crazy vision, he builds a baseball field with bleachers and floodlights right in the middle of a cornfield outside of Dyersville. Sometimes one can get too much sun out there in a hot Iowa cornfield in the middle of the season. But this isn't a case of sunstroke.

The voice was right. People do come, including the ghosts of Shoeless Joe Jackson and other White Sox players disgraced in the 1919 baseball scandal. They emerge from the steamy cornfields to play a few games on the Field of Dreams that Ray has built. At one point in the film, Shoeless Joe asks, "Is this heaven?" Ray (and every Iowan in the audience) replies, "No, it's Iowa."

Sometimes, I think libraries are like Ray Kinsella. We build it, hoping that people will come, without knowing exactly what we are building, or precisely who will be coming.

Lizabeth A. Wilson is Director of University Libraries, University of Washington, Seattle, WA (E-mail: betsyw@u.washington.edu).

[Haworth co-indexing entry note]: "If We Build It, Will They Come? Library Users in a Digital World." Wilson, Lizabeth A. Co-published simultaneously in *Journal of Library Administration* (The Haworth Information Press, an imprint of The Haworth Press, Inc.) Vol. 39, No. 4, 2003, pp. 19-28; and: *Improved Access to Information: Portals, Content Selection, and Digital Information* (ed: Sul H. Lee) The Haworth Information Press, an imprint of The Haworth Press, Inc., 2003, pp. 19-28. Single or multiple copies of this article are available for a fee from The Haworth Document Delivery Service [1-800-HAWORTH, 9:00 a.m. - 5:00 p.m. (EST). E-mail address: docdelivery@haworthpress.com].

http://www.haworthpress.com/web/JLA
© 2003 by The Haworth Press, Inc. All rights reserved.
Digital Object Identifier: 10.1300/J111v39n04_03

This paper addresses how to build a better Field of Information Dreams–one that is inextricably interwoven with user needs and preferences in a digital world. I will highlight recent usage studies, suggest some effective assessment and usability approaches, and conclude with a discussion of the need for institutional research agendas.

Since portals are a theme of this volume and of the conference at which this paper was originally delivered, I cannot resist an introductory aside. I am not convinced that the term portal is particularly meaningful for describing our aspirations.

Maybe it's only my problem. When I hear the term portal, I conjure up images of a door. Doors invoke many associations, including the "Let's Make a Deal" doors from my television-watching childhood in Iowa.

Game host Monte Hall encourages the contestants to "pick a door." Will it be door number one, number two, or number three? The excitement builds as we wait to see if they win a car, a vacation, or a vacuum cleaner. Likewise, pick a portal from myriad portals. The excitement builds as we wait to see where the connection takes us. To an online catalog, a digital repository, or a dead link?

Lorcan Dempsey's approach to portals is particularly helpful, and I will use his definition as a basis for this paper. Dempsey describes portals as creating environments which are useful and efficient for users as they engage with information and knowledge resources and experts. Dempsey provides a useful and elegant framing of portals. It is the execution that is so challenging.

RECENT USER STUDIES

For many years we lacked sufficient broad-based user studies to guide our investment in resources and staff used to create useful environments. There have been the occasional catalog use studies, the less frequent disciplinary studies, and the more common institutionally based use studies ("how we did it good"). By and large, we have been on our own as we built environments often predicated solely on local experience, anecdotal evidence, and good intentions.

Over the past year there has been a significant investment in documenting the information-seeking behaviors of our collective users. Three recent major reports should be on everybody's reading and action list.

OCLC published a white paper in June 2002 on the information habits of college students.[1] The study concentrated on the web-based information habits of 1,050 college students and their use of campus library websites. The studies found that students look to campus libraries and library websites for their information needs, but were confounded by numerous barriers.

Students were frustrated by:

- Inability to access databases remotely due to password requirements and license restrictions
- Difficulty searching and navigating within the library and its website
- Costs of copying and printing at the library
- Shortage of knowledgeable librarians
- Lack of the customer service they have come to expect as consumers

Students particularly were frustrated by the awareness that libraries have more information than they could make or would make available remotely. Students reported a performance gap between their expectations for service and their perceptions about the service they receive.

The report makes several salient recommendations to be considered as we build that field of information dreams:

- Emphasize the common preferences of students and librarians for accuracy, authority, timeliness, and privacy
- Tightly integrate the library's electronic resources with the campus website
- Enable open access for remote users
- Offer clear and readily available navigational guides–both online and onsite
- Provide relentless promotion, instruction, and customer service

In 2002, the Digital Library Federation and Council on Library and Information Resources commissioned Outsell, Inc. to conduct an extensive national survey of campus users of scholarly information.[2] The survey involved over 3,200 faculty, graduate students and undergraduates in nearly 400 institutions. While the results are still being distilled, interpreted, and disseminated, we already have gained several insights from this study, including:

- Users feel comfortable with electronic resources
- Users use electronic resources, quite confidently
- Onsite library use remains substantial, but is changing as libraries themselves develop digital content, online services, and in-house computer facilities

As with the OCLC study, academic library users in the Outsell survey report problems and barriers, including:

- Having enough time
- Knowing what's available
- Having access to all information from one place
- Determining information quality, credibility, and accuracy
- Having sufficient training on how to search for information

In Outsell's opinion, these barriers fall within the domain of libraries to address. Libraries can help users become more effective in their information searching through more intuitive products and information environments, and information literacy efforts.

In September 2002, the Pew Internet and American Life Project published *The Internet Goes to College: How Student Are Living in the Future with Today's Technology*.[3] While this report does not focus solely on library use as the Outsell and OCLC surveys do, it provides a compelling picture of 2,000 students at 27 institutions. The Pew study summarizes its findings:

- College students are early adopters and heavy users of the Internet
- Students say that the Internet has enhanced their education
- College social life has been changed by the Internet

While those who work with students might not find these findings new or insightful, the magnitude and stickiness of these changes cannot be underestimated.

These three studies combine to give a rich understanding of user preferences, readiness, and behaviors that we can use as we create information environments. In addition, it behooves us to look ahead to the next generation of academic library users.

As one illustration, consider Microsoft's NetGen project.[4] Thirty-something Microsoft employee Tammy Savage told her bosses about the 13-24 year-old set. She said, "They are on instant messenger before their morning coffee." (I guess in caffeine-enabled Seattle it is okay to drink coffee when you are 13.) If Microsoft wanted to be relevant in the future, she told them, it had to adjust to the Networked Generation, even if it meant producing software that the middle-aged guys didn't embrace.

In 2000 she had the chance to test her perceptions by observing twelve undergraduates living in a big house in Seattle for three weeks. She instructed them that their job was to develop a business plan for a new company. What she really cared about was the way they used technology to communicate with each other as they cooked up dot.com schemes.

What did she learn and what should be taken away from the experiment? Savage found that to the Networked Generation technology is an environment, not a tool. These students used the Net to socialize and build relationships.

Out of this experience, Savage fostered *threedegrees*, a new product whose essence is relationships. *Threedegrees* is half the amount of the alleged six degrees of separation allotted to any two randomly chosen people. *Threedegrees* relies on peer-to-peer technology and enables communication. For the purposes of this paper, the technology behind *threedegrees* is not what is important. It is relevant to understand that for future academic library users, it is no longer about portals, software, information resources. For these users, it is about dynamic and flexible environments which support interaction and relationships. There's a lesson in *threedegrees* as we build our field of dreams.

ASSESSMENT

While broad-based user studies provide us with a framework for decision-making, we need to understand our local environments and user preferences as we build out our local offering. We need to build substantive assessment frameworks, infrastructures, and expertise.

In the early '90s under the leadership of then Library Director Betty Bengtson, the University of Washington Libraries made a commitment to becoming a user-centered enterprise. We needed to explicitly define who our users were in order to determine if we were meeting their needs. We needed to be positioned to make the best use of diminishing resources, to select the best from a growing array of options, and to market services realistically. Most importantly, we needed to engage both staff and users in a decision-making dialog on what new services, collections, information formats, and programs would be introduced and what they will no longer do or provide.

Now nearly a decade later, we continue to nurture our "culture of assessment" and dedicate resources to gathering and mining robust data about users and their information needs as we shape the "any time any place" library. We systematically use multiple assessment methods, including triennial surveys, focus groups, in-library surveys, LibQual, usability testing, and use statistics, to create a robust multi-dimensional perspective on our diverse user community.

We have focused our assessment efforts on gaining a better understanding of how online information resources and services impact the work of our users. In general, our assessment efforts show that our community of faculty and students is moving rapidly to remote use of online information. Indeed, it is the preferred method for finding and using information needed for work.

We also have unearthed several principles that guide the development of our information field of dreams. For instance, self-reliance and the ability to perform library-related work without staff mediation are of high importance to our users. Information technology and online information resources enable faculty and students to be more productive. Faculty, graduate students, and undergraduates all rank the desktop delivery of full-text and full-image resources as their highest priority for the Libraries. Undergraduates continue to use libraries as a place to do work, but the frequency of faculty and graduate student use of physical facilities continues to drop, most notably in those units that have large journal collections. The Libraries remain important for the work of students. Indeed, the importance of the UW Libraries to undergraduates increased between 1998 and 2002 while the importance of the Web declined.

Two focus groups were held in spring 2002, centered on the topic of the impact of online library resources on faculty and student work. The faculty and graduate students groups were comprised primarily of people from health sciences and the sciences. Some of the comments that arose independently in each group included:

- Google is the initial search starting point for many searches
- Bibliographic database interfaces are too complex
- Color is critical and color printers are in wide use
- Electronic journals foster ubiquity of library research, any place, any time
- Fewer visits to the library equals greater efficiency
- Personal connection to library staff is important

There were many common discussion threads in the focus groups. They tell the story of the impact of online resources and information technology in the words of our faculty and graduate students.

One graduate student from the biosciences remarked:

I wish all my journals were online. It's not so much that I dislike trekking to different libraries, it's just the whole process of getting there, tracking down the journal, finding a working copy machine. It's just so time-consuming and I have so little time. I have no time.

A faculty member commented on how electronic resources had changed her research patterns:

I find that it has changed the way I do library research. It used to be a stage process: initial trip, follow-up trip, fine-tuning trip. Now it's continuous iterative thing. I can follow-up at any time.

We continuously use our data banks for decision-making, priority setting, planning, and policy development, and make the full reports and data available for others to consult on our web site.[5] During the next two years, we will continue to develop a multi-faceted assessment program, focus on outcomes-based assessment, develop measures for the virtual library, and establish a central data and analysis site.

FROM VISION TO TRANSFORMATION

In addition to our assessment planning for the near future, we are engaged in a watershed initiative with humanities and social science scholars to help shape a new model of academic support for digital scholarship. Thanks to a generous gift from the Andrew Mellon Foundation, we have launched an initiative entitled: "From Vision to Transformation: New Models of Academic Support for Digital Scholarship."[6] In March 2003, we brought together 40 scholars, 10 technology, library, and academic planners, and 5 external experts at the Sleeping Lady Mountain Retreat in the Cascade Mountains of Washington state to engage in questions surrounding what academic support is needed for digital scholarship. Two questions guided the retreat:

- As a scholar, what are your needs and wants with regard to digital scholarship, collections, and technologies?
- What strategies should the University and the Libraries take to advance such scholarship and learning?

Following the retreat, we are developing a plan that enables the UW, its library, and other like-minded institutions to support individual scholars and communities to advance research and instruction, especially in the humanities and social sciences. While we cannot predict what elements will emerge as next steps, we can speculate that the model will be collaborative, global, integrative, and multi-disciplinary. We anticipate that a D-Space-like infrastructure will be a critical component of any institution-wide architecture. We also envision that our geographic location, regional alliances, and international relationships will influence our particular take. The model of academic support for digital scholarship inevitably will reach beyond the Pacific Northwest.

USABILITY TESTING

We are using available user studies and research, our local assessment efforts, and focused initiatives such as the Mellon effort to make the wisest investments in creating environments in which users thrive. But a critical question remains. If they get there, can they make their way around the environments we have created?

Simplicity is the silver spike, and usability testing is the hammer. Most libraries acknowledge the value of usability testing, but fewer have integrated usability into operations. While our emphasis on assessment grew over the past decade, it has only been in the last few years that we have committed substantive resources to building a usability capacity. We have opened a usability lab in the library, established a graduate assistant position devoted to usability, and developed a master plan.[7]

RESEARCH AGENDAS

Has the research, assessment, and usability testing helped us build a better information environment? Yes, without a doubt. However, a major element is missing–an articulated research agenda.

To help address compelling research questions, I depend on the good work of the OCLC Office of Research, the Digital Library Federation, CLIR, and library and information science schools. I recognize that the Association of College and Research Libraries Focus on the Future Effort has outlined some of the big questions for the field.[8] Dagobert Soergel framed a vision for digital library research.[9] However, individual libraries cannot abdicate their responsibility to create a local research agenda. Libraries will launch new initiatives even in tight budget times. To the extent that a research agenda can support strategic initiatives or help avoid expensive mistakes, it becomes an investment in our collective future.

Libraries, either individually or collectively, need to create a research agenda. We are attempting to do so at the University of Washington. Our approach has been informed by a white paper developed by William Jordan, Acting Associate Director of Libraries for Library Systems, University of Washington.

In his paper, Jordan asks, "Why is a research agenda critical at this juncture?" He posits:

> We know that undergraduates exhibit different information-seeking behaviors than do graduate students or faculty, and we have long recognized the existence of disciplinary-based differences in how users acquire and use information. We have shaped our services and collections to accommodate those differences. But there have been sweeping changes in how users can interact with information, and the impact of those changes is not well understood.

> Are there, for example, differences emerging between communities that rely on "surrogate-based access" for resource discovery versus those that are able to access information objects directly that are equally profound? How are users coping with the quantity, variety, and variable quality of information resources? What does this mean for our services and collections?[10]

The research agenda complements our assessment and usability work. For example, assessment tends to measure how well we have met user needs, current user behavior, and perceptions. Questions following from assessment data can, and should, suggest elements of the research agenda.

Usability testing focuses on how well users can complete a task with a given tool or interface. As with assessment data, usability testing can surface items for the research agenda as well as provide useful protocols for particular types of research questions.

What we are proposing is an institutional rather than an individual research agenda, and one that focuses on applied as opposed to wholly theoretical research. The Libraries' research enterprise must have a strong connection to strategic goals. We will concentrate on questions surrounding user information-seeking behavior, questions surrounding major new initiatives, and questions surrounding high cost/high effort ongoing activities, such as our strategic focus on creating the "any time any place" library. Identifying what questions we need answered in order to move forward is the first step, and one in which we are encouraging broad participation.

SUMMARY

In conclusion, I return to the title of this paper and ask "If we build it, will they come?" By leveraging what we learn from user studies, assessment and usability efforts, and institutional research, we can build information environments that are useful and efficient for users. When we ask our users what they need, nurture relationships, and scour the research, we must commit to doing something with what we have learned.

When we succeed in creating environments that are authentic, intuitive, integrated, and transparent, our users will step out of the cornfields onto our Field of Dreams and ask, "Is this Heaven?" We will be able to say, "No, it's the Library."

REFERENCES

1. *OCLC White Paper on the Information Habits of College Students* (2002). URL: http://www2.oclc.org/oclc/pdf/printondemand/informationhabits.pdf.

2. *Dimensions and Use of the Scholarly Information Environment: Introduction to a Data Set Assembled by the Digital Library Federation and Outsell, Inc.* (2002). URL: <http://www.clir.org/pubs/abstract/pub110abst.html>.

3. *The Internet Goes to College: How Student Are Living in the Future with Today's Technolog.* URL: http://www.pewinternet.org/reports/pdfs/PIP_College_Report.pdf.

4. "Microsoft gets a Clue from its Kiddie Corps," *Newsweek* (February 24, 2003): 56-57.

5. University of Washington Libraries Assessment. URL: <http://www.lib.washington.edu/assessment/>.

6. From Vision to Transformation: New Models of Academic Support for Digital Scholarship. URL: <http://www.lib.washington.edu/digitalscholar/>.

7. UW Library Systems: Web Usability, <http://staffweb.lib.washington.edu/usability/>.

8. Hisle, W. Lee, "Top Issues Facing Academic Libraries: A Report of the Focus on the Future Task Force," *C&RL News* (November 2002).

9. Soergel, Dagobert, "A Framework for Digital Library Research," *D-Lib Magazine* (December 2002). URL: <http://www.dlib.org/dlib/december02/soergel/12soergel.html>.

10. Jordan, William. 2003. "Creating a Research Agenda for the UW Libraries."

Ties That Bind:
Non-Technological Measures
for Promoting Persistent Access
to Knowledge Resources

Bernard F. Reilly, Jr.

My talk today stems from some of CRL's programmatic and strategic planning activities over the past year. CRL is a cooperative framework for building and managing resources for advanced scholarly research. More concretely, the Center is a consortium of about 200 North American research libraries, most of them academic. CRL collects and builds resources for advanced research in the humanities, sciences, and social sciences, and makes them available to scholars through member libraries. Hence persistent access is a topic of serious concern for us.

The challenges of ensuring the long-term accessibility, or persistence, of digital resources are largely technological. Solutions to these challenges will require reconciling the inherently dynamic and mercurial characteristics of digital objects (and the technologies that support them) with the permanence that is the goal of preservation.

But aside from this daunting technological challenge there is another level on which persistence needs to be supported. Persistence on this other level affects digital and traditional resources alike. This is the level of the organizational and economic framework within which the various parties who support the survival of the resources in question operate. Certain organizational and

---

Bernard F. Reilly, Jr., is President, The Center for Research Libraries, Chicago, IL.

[Haworth co-indexing entry note]: "Ties That Bind: Non-Technological Measures for Promoting Persistent Access to Knowledge Resources." Reilly, Bernard F., Jr. Co-published simultaneously in *Journal of Library Administration* (The Haworth Information Press, an imprint of The Haworth Press, Inc.) Vol. 39, No. 4, 2003, pp. 29-39; and: *Improved Access to Information: Portals, Content Selection, and Digital Information* (ed: Sul H. Lee) The Haworth Information Press, an imprint of The Haworth Press, Inc., 2003, pp. 29-39. Single or multiple copies of this article are available for a fee from The Haworth Document Delivery Service [1-800-HAWORTH, 9:00 a.m. - 5:00 p.m. (EST). E-mail address: docdelivery@haworthpress.com].

http://www.haworthpress.com/web/JLA
© 2003 by The Haworth Press, Inc. All rights reserved.
Digital Object Identifier: 10.1300/J111v39n04_04

governance structures can promote persistence, and certain kinds of economic models are better suited than others to minimizing risk and ensuring the appropriate stewardship of resources.

Preservation of digital resources then requires more than technological ingenuity; it requires the right kind of organizational structures, accountability, and control that support the resources developed.

Today's brief report stems from three studies undertaken in connection with an analysis of CRL's own cooperative model:

1. Cooperative Collection Development–a survey of the ways various CCD projects control risk
2. Cooperative Print Management–a study of cooperative collection management efforts developed as part of inter-institutional print depositories, and their governance and economic models
3. Cooperative Web Archiving–an examination of the merits of various prospective organizational models and distribution of activities for the cooperative archiving of Web-based political communications.

All three types of endeavors involve multiple participants, usually libraries, or multiple communities, like academic communities, acting upon a common pool of resources. All require organizational and economic structures and mechanisms that enable the development and management of those resources. These structures and mechanisms present varying degrees of risks and varying degrees of stability. In the peculiar physics of cooperation, as in natural-world physics, some structures are inherently more stable than others; some are prone to endure and to continue to support equitable access to resources and others vulnerable to favor the interests of only a few.

I will sketch out briefly what we've learned from each of these three projects in turn, and hope to convince you that this adds up to something, that in the end there is a common thread.

COOPERATIVE COLLECTION DEVELOPMENT–
RELATIONSHIPS AND AGREEMENTS

In preparation for the Center's conference last November on cooperative collection development, we looked at a range of CCD projects and programs in the research library sector. Our inquiry focused on projects that developed traditional print collections and/or digital library collections. These activities involved partnerships among libraries, universities, publishers, and other organizations that joined together to acquire or, in the case of digital, create collections of research materials.

Activities undertaken by these projects included creating an online library of primary source materials in digital form contributed by multiple institutions, as was accomplished under the Library of Congress/Ameritech National Digital Library Competition project. Others entailed the sharing of responsibility for comprehensive collecting in a particular domain, such as the Research Library Cooperative Acquisition Program in Latin American Materials undertaken by the University of Texas, Stanford University and the University of California at Berkeley.

Such activities entail the shared investment of resources, the allocation of specific roles and responsibilities to the participants, and the timely fulfillment of those responsibilities. The roles and responsibilities may be short-term commitments, fulfilled during a specified, limited time period. Or they may be ongoing commitments, undertaken for long or even indefinite periods of time.

These activities, moreover, normally involve a sharing of ownership in the resources collectively developed. More broadly, this involves apportioning to each participant an interest or share in the potential benefits of the project. This interest is the participant's equity stake in the benefits of a resource. Depending on the kind of collection or resource developed this share could translate to physical possession of an object or collection, the right to modify a digital resource developed, or the ability to access an electronic subscription. This interest, though, might also go beyond the actual resources developed and include other returns on investment, such as compensatory payments arising from a vendor's breach of supply or license agreements, or royalties or fees derived from permissible "downstream" uses of the resource controlled by the group.

Conversely, risk is also shared among participants in CCD projects. Participating libraries can be exposed to losses that might arise from negative consequences and scenarios stemming from those activities. Such costs might include the loss of a party's investment because of procurement failure or fraud on the part of an agent or vendor, purchase or delivery cost overruns, substantial unforeseen price increases, or even monetary penalties and damages from copyright infringement or a project participant's breach of a vendor contract. In collection development activity, however, the major cost incurred is usually the cost of long-term maintenance, or preservation, of the acquired resource.

The study analyzed the numerous ways in which risk enters into cooperative collection development activities, and indicated broadly some measures that can be taken in those activities to enable this risk to be more effectively minimized. The paper that came out of the study will be published as part of the Aberdeen Woods Conference published proceedings. I will only summarize here three characteristics of CCD projects that minimize risk and thereby better ensure longevity for the resources developed.

Relationships and Agreements

Formality and Clear Allocation of Risk. In cooperative endeavors, contracts and formal agreements serve the function of abating risk by distributing the costs of potential losses from the endeavor, apportioning the potential costs and liabilities that might accrue among the investing parties. This is done so that in the event of a loss no single party bears an unduly large share of the total damages. Such instruments also serve to apportion benefits *among* the parties as well; promoting a clear understanding of the equity that each holds in the resource. In the commercial sector similar development activities tend to be supported contractually. A robust infrastructure consisting of written cooperative agreements, licenses, and the other documents underpin and specify the roles and commitments of contributors, vendors, beneficiaries, and other participants in joint ventures. This infrastructure rests upon a base of contract law and commercial code that govern transactions and trade in the larger economy. Such an apparatus is intended to provide a "safety net" of sorts that underwrites the processes of collaboration and exchange, and enables participants to limit and manage the various risks associated with these processes.

Unfortunately many CCD projects are memorialized by memoranda of understanding, letters of intent, and other non-binding documents. Contracts and other truly binding agreements are rare. This creates the potential for ambiguity about ownership or control of the resource, which could ultimately have a "paralyzing" effect, preventing decisions critical to preservation of the resource from being made or the responsibility to preserve it from being enforced.

The parties identified in such agreements, moreover, need to be legal entities, i.e., specifically identified individuals or legally vested corporations. In the eyes of the law, liability cannot accrue to, nor can obligations be enforced of, an ad hoc or arbitrarily designated entity such as a "project" or a team. Projects and teams have no legal standing per se: they cannot own property nor possess rights. They also come and go with none of the mechanisms that ensure continuity of ownership and responsibility for legal entities. When the parties to an agreement are either not clearly identified, or are not specifically empowered to enter into a contract as representatives of a legal entity, the value of the contract and the usual protections of the law can be compromised. Here again the maintenance of a resource or collection can be undermined. When the parties are so defined it becomes easier to scrutinize their reliability and hence distinguish between trustworthy and unreliable parties.

The fortunes of the members of the American research libraries community are interlinked. Informal, voluntary cooperation among libraries, for instance, occurs in the efforts of libraries to avoid the unnecessary development of redundant resources. Interlibrary loan and Web dissemination enable unique collection resources developed by one library to be shared by others.

Because of this inter-reliance, the collecting decisions of one library often influence the behavior of others active in the same area. In this way libraries not directly participating in a cooperative collection effort can still have a real interest or stake in that effort's success. A library might rely upon another to collect or preserve unique materials or materials only available by virtue of a temporary window of opportunity. It can then make a great deal of difference to this larger community, for instance, how securely or for how long a party is bound to fulfill its obligations to a cooperative effort. The consequences of "courses not taken" can be dire.

When the specific terms of a cooperative endeavor are unclear, or are altogether unknown, the other actors and, to a lesser extent, even the participating parties are deprived of useful knowledge on which to base important acquisition or preservation decisions. In the absence of information all stakeholders then operate at a higher level of risk. Risk to other interested parties can be mitigated somewhat by transparency. Currently our collection development activities, particularly the development of electronic resources, are not very transparent. Few cooperative agreements that underwrite projects and programs, even major ones, are published. Hence we are often unable to calculate the risk of relying on others' performance of manifest responsibilities in a program or project.[1]

Librarians are obliged to manage carefully the financial and human resources at their disposal. And the prudent management of knowledge resources is also a fiduciary responsibility. This makes it necessary for us to put into place whatever measures we can to minimize risk.

We now move on to the realm of cooperative collection management.

COOPERATIVE COLLECTION MANAGEMENT–
INTER-INSTITUTIONAL DEPOSITORIES

While institutions join together to build resources through cooperative collection *development*, inter-institutional depositories, like the Five College Depository Library and the regional library facilities of California and Ohio, involve cooperative *management* of resources that have already been developed. Depositories provide a distinct category of access in line with the kinds of materials they manage: they provide a solution for storage and delivery of low-use materials: humanities and social science books and serials, newspapers, materials available electronically or in microform, foreign language materials.

In the depositories, collections owned by separate institutions are brought together under one roof, and subjected to common conditions and regimens regarding processing, loan, handling, and access. In some depositories the collections are even subjected to a common management regime as if they were part of a single collection, which includes minimization and elimination of duplication and their development incorporated into a unified, coordinated strategy. In rare cases they are even merged into a single collection, whose ownership is shared among contributing libraries. In every case the depositories represent a shared financial investment and the undertaking by the various participants of specific roles and responsibilities.

In this study we also looked at collections of record, including the Library of Congress and the American Antiquarian Society. While this in some respects mixes apples and oranges, these do share with the regional depositories the function of preserving materials upon which others rely. LC and the AAS fulfill fall-back collecting and preservation responsibilities for a range of materials–early American imprints, newspapers, area studies materials and others–for the larger library community.

In surveying the depositories we were interested in how far the participating libraries had gone to merge collection management activities, in order to determine to what extent their regional efforts could be linked, or built upon, to achieve broader, nationwide cooperation in managing printed knowledge resources. Here it was the governance and financial structures of the depositories that most interested us. These seemed to have a pronounced effect on the preservation of collections of record or cooperative collection management in depositories. And they would be essential building blocks for any national effort.

We found that some governance and financial models adopted by the depositories are more conducive to supporting long-term availability to the community of the resources that they manage. I'll sketch this out briefly.

Governance Models. We found a range of governance models, almost as many as there are depositories. All have their benefits, and those benefits have an effect on their programs, and ultimately on their ability to provide long-term access for the broader community.

Single-Institution Repository Model. Here a single institution preserves and manages collections on behalf of a larger community but is organizationally independent of that community. Overall programmatic direction is given by a Board of Directors/Trustees or governing body. This model's drawback is that the program will most likely be shaped by the interests of the governing body, whose interests are not necessarily congruent with those of the community that relies upon the repository. (The Library of Congress is such a repository, for instance, whose governing body, the U.S. Congress, has a broad spectrum of interests that compete at times with the needs of the nation's other libraries.)

The management of those materials, moreover, is determined by the internal collection development and preservation aims of the organization, which are formalized through collection development policies. These aims may be, but are not necessarily bound to be, responsive to the priorities of the other libraries in the community since ultimate accountability is to the governing body.

System-Wide Depositories. Some of the collection management endeavors are mandated by the governing authority of the community, e.g., a state university system, in response to system needs. The governing authority sets the general program of the endeavor, which can involve maintenance of a facility, a cooperative collecting program, or even digital resource development. With the inter-institutional depositories, the ongoing program is determined by a governing body that is formally, usually legally accountable to the members of the system. Given the makeup of the board, specifically the active involvement at the highest system level, there is likelihood that the facilities' programs will be tied to system-wide strategies and priorities.

Consortium Model. Here participating libraries or universities join together in a broader endeavor mandated by the university or college at the president's level. These consortia normally include a wide range of common educational and infrastructure programs, including curriculum sharing, of which the collections management endeavor is a subset. The activities of the consortium can be fused under the broader educational and institutions goals set by university presidents, or shaped by the interests of the libraries within those universities. The governing bodies of such consortia are normally drawn from the president or university administration-level of the participating institution, from the university library directors, or from both.

Within the consortium the common interests of the participating libraries are likely to prevail, unless the degree of influence participants wield is unequal. Such inequality can stem from imbalances arising from the funding models (discussed below) or from the inevitability that certain parties will take more active roles in program development or policymaking than others. Such imbalances can often be offset by pre-established written policies designed to "level the playing field."

Funding Models. The sources and nature of the funding that underwrites the inter-institutional repositories can have a decided effect on those repositories' programs. It can also influence the extent and nature of participation by member libraries. We examined three basic types of funding models.

"Entitlement" Funding. Here capital and operating funds for the depository are provided either directly by the governing authority, i.e., the federal or state government, or by a university system. The facilities budget allocation is determined on the basis of demand from participating libraries. Under this model the individual participants do not pay a share of the operating costs, but may pay surcharges based on extra services. Participation in this instance often needs to be incentivized by quotas or other means to realize optimum occupancy.

Even Allocation. This model involves an even division of capital and/or operating costs among the participating institutions, with surcharges often linked to services provided in addition to storage. The system encourages use of the facility by not penalizing the heavy users, but is probably not scalable. The economic base in such a model would not be responsive to increases in demand by some participants without rendering low users' contributions non cost-effective.

Acreage System. Here operating and capital costs are apportioned according to an actual or anticipated volume count or amount of space expected to be occupied by the participants' collections. The annual contribution of each participant is set at a percentage of costs proportionate to the actual or anticipated amount of material included in the facility by that participant. The participants' fees must be adjusted frequently enough to keep up with their changing occupancy, but not so frequently as to undermine their ability to plan long-term budgets. The drawback of this model is that it does not promote long-term commitment to support of the depository itself, and hence participants are less likely to support necessary capital improvements in the depository.

Hence a range of models, none of them inherently faulty, support varying but acceptable kinds of outcomes. Now, let's move on from the realm of print and paper to the digital realm.

COOPERATIVE WEB ARCHIVING: WEB-BASED POLITICAL COMMUNICATIONS

This program is only recently underway. It involves thinking about the organizational structures and partnerships necessary to enable a sustainable set of activities. CRL's initiative, funded by the Andrew W. Mellon Foundation, aims to promote long-term survival of the important documents and messages disseminated via the World Wide Web by non-governmental political organizations and groups. These materials provide a valuable source of information for historical studies and the social sciences, but are by nature fugitive and susceptible to loss. We hope to lay the groundwork for cooperative preservation of political Web content by the research library community. Participating in the effort are four universities–Cornell University, New York University, Stanford University, and the University of Texas at Austin–and the San Francisco-based Internet Archive.

The effort will produce a framework and general specifications for three aspects of ongoing, sustainable archiving:

1. *Long-Term Resource Management*–The organizational and economic framework needed to support archiving, management, and preservation of Web political materials on an ongoing, cooperative basis.

2. *Curatorship*–The optimal curatorial regimes and practices for identification, targeting and capture of Web political communications to be archived.
3. *Technology*–The general technical requirements, specifications, and tools best suited to the capture and archiving of political communications.

I will focus here on the long-term resource management part. We first defined a set of activities that support archiving the political Web. These range from prospecting for archives content and content selection, to indexing and metadata production, to quality assurance and rights management.

One question is how to organize these activities to achieve the highest likelihood that the resources will persist and remain available to the community. Some of these are core activities and should be undertaken centrally. Who are the appropriate participants in these activities and why? Which activities should be performed centrally and which distributed? Where would those archiving activities take place? What is the right distribution to support accountability?

Ideally, the tools, methodologies, and management structures employed by the archives will enable both centralized and local activities:

1. *Centralized or Core Activities*–To achieve economies of scale needed to support the archives some activities will necessarily be centralized, i.e., undertaken or controlled centrally to ensure the integrity and persistence of the common resource. It might be most effective (both in terms of cost and effort) to centrally develop common procedures, tools, policies, and standards. Centralized programming and development would be advisable, as this is usually the most costly activity.
2. *Local or Voluntary Activities*–To counterbalance somewhat the force of the centralized organization, certain activities would be undertaken locally but would augment the common resource, in conformance to standards and policies, but performed locally by individuals on an informal or voluntary basis. The selection activities are probably best distributed rather than centralized, and undertaken at universities and centers where specific region or language-based expertise is supported. This can take advantage of existing region, language, or subject-based activities such as portal-building or traditional collecting. Content might also be harvested from that collected by third party knowledge-producing organizations like the World Bank, Amnesty International, and others that archive materials for their own purposes.

In identifying appropriate participants, accountability and efficiency were the prevailing principles. To ensure inclusion in the archives of the most important political Web content, individual scholars, historians, and other specialists in the field should be involved in selection and, to the extent possible, other archiving activities. The anticipated uses of the archives also include study and informational use by members of the international development, policy, diplomatic, and journalism communities and by lay individuals. Hence, to ensure the utility of the resource to this audience, institutes and other non-profit knowledge organizations, foundations, government bodies, and their agents might also take part in the archiving endeavor.

The high level of sophistication and standardization required in the work of generating and maintaining such archives over the long term, and the importance of such archives as a resource for the larger scholarly community, suggest that this is not just a peer-to-peer activity. At minimum, then, some mechanism for certification of participating individuals will probably have to be provided. And mission-critical activities like standards, economic infrastructure, quality control, and others will have to be undertaken under the control of the libraries.

We considered the thorny question of whether the original producers or hosts of political Web content should be involved in archiving activities as well. The consensus was that they should be consulted on their willingness to permit inclusion of their content in the common resource. However, if deep Web material is eventually to be included in the archives, cooperation from creators of some sites will be needed to enable retrieval of material and circumvention of technical protections like robot exclusions, password protection.

Other kinds of organizations, such as publishers, aggregators, others that offer ready channels of distribution and/or robust existing financial or subscription capabilities necessary to the archiving effort might play a role as contractors or vendors. But the way in which copyrights are handled will affect the eligibility of some to participate in the archiving. Federal agencies like the Library of Congress and for-profit organizations, for instance, are extremely risk-averse with regard to copyright and therefore require greater "insulation" from copyright liabilities than others.

Moreover, copyright restrictions apply differently to each activity. For instance, the highest risk associated with copyright infringement will inure to the access- and distribution-related activities. Conversely, risk will be lower for those engaged in curation and "dark" archiving activities. This might require some creative "partitioning" among the activities to insulate parties from harm.

To close these meanderings across three very divergent areas of endeavor, I want to point out a thread common to all. Essential to the persistent availability of digital and printed resources to the larger community is the soundness of the organizational, economic and legal infrastructure of cooperative resource management. Today those at work in the library world have to manage a more complex array of printed and electronic resources than ever before in a highly fluid, transitional environment. This non-technological infrastructure will be key to the successful shift from print to electronic resources, and will yield benefits in both realms.

NOTE

1. The Elsevier Science-National Library of the Netherlands electronic journals archiving agreement, cited above, potentially has a significant bearing on the security of a large and valuable shared resource and on the print archiving decisions of many libraries invested in the resource. The text of the agreement was not readily available for inspection as of this writing.

Knowledge Management in Academic Libraries: Building the Knowledge Bank at the Ohio State University

Joseph J. Branin

INTRODUCTION:
AN EVOLUTION TOWARDS KNOWLEDGE MANAGEMENT

As I survey the field of collection management over the last fifty years, I see an evolution in its history that can be characterized as a movement from "collection development," to "collection management," to present day "knowledge management." I have already described this evolution several times in writing and in presentations,[1] but in summary let me give you my perspective both as a participant in (as a bibliographer and collection development officer) and observer of (as a library administrator) this evolution over the last half century.

The Collection Development Era

Libraries in North America expanded rapidly in the post-World War II and post-sputnik era of 1950 to 1975. If you were lucky enough to have been a bib-

Joseph J. Branin is Director of Libraries, Ohio State University Libraries, Columbus, OH (E-mail: branin.1@osu.edu).

[Haworth co-indexing entry note]: "Knowledge Management in Academic Libraries: Building the Knowledge Bank at the Ohio State University." Branin, Joseph J. Co-published simultaneously in *Journal of Library Administration* (The Haworth Information Press, an imprint of The Haworth Press, Inc.) Vol. 39, No. 4, 2003, pp. 41-56; and: *Improved Access to Information: Portals, Content Selection, and Digital Information* (ed: Sul H. Lee) The Haworth Information Press, an imprint of The Haworth Press, Inc., 2003, pp. 41-56. Single or multiple copies of this article are available for a fee from The Haworth Document Delivery Service [1-800-HAWORTH, 9:00 a.m. - 5:00 p.m. (EST). E-mail address: docdelivery@haworthpress.com].

http://www.haworthpress.com/web/JLA
© 2003 by The Haworth Press, Inc. All rights reserved.
Digital Object Identifier: 10.1300/J111v39n04_05

liographer in a research library during this era, you were likely to be spending most of your time acquiring material to build collections as quickly as you possibly could. It was the era of scouring in-print and out-of-print book vendor catalogs, clearing out the inventories of book stores, raiding foreign libraries, and international book buying trips. Print material, in the form of books, journals, and manuscripts, was pretty much the exclusive, or at least the predominant, medium for library acquisitions during this "collection development" period. (I unfortunately did not become a bibliographer until 1977, but my institution at the time, the University of Georgia, was still greatly expanding its library holdings, and I experienced the tail end of this exhilarating time of collection development and building.)

The Collection Management Era

Over the next twenty-five years, from roughly 1975 to 2000, the conditions for and nature of collection development changed. The money flowed less freely; the cost of library material, particularly the cost of journal subscriptions in science and technology, rose more quickly than library budgets; and, of course, something of an information technology revolution occurred. I characterize this period as one that emphasized "management" over "development" in the collections field of librarianship. Nineteen seventy-nine was a banner year for the emerging collection management field. The American Library Association first issued *Guidelines for Collection Development*, which began to codify the practice of collection development and management, and the two most important and influential studies of resource development and use in research libraries were published: Charles Osburn's *Academic Research and Libraries Resources: Changing Patterns in America* and Allen Kent's *Use of Library Materials: The University of Pittsburgh Study*.[2] Essentially, what Osburn and Kent told us was that we had to pay more attention to the changing information needs and habits of American scholars and scientists as we built research library collections.

In 1981, the American Library Association sponsored its first institute on collection development and management at Stanford University, and Paul Mosher, then head of collections at Stanford University Libraries (he is now University Librarian at the University of Pennsylvania), offered the keynote address entitled "Fighting Back: From Collection Development to Collection Management."[3] What Mosher described was a shift in emphasis from building research collections in a seemingly comprehensive or indiscriminate fashion to one of careful analysis, prudent acquisitions, and management of scarce resources. Collection management emerged as a more complete and balanced approach to the collections arena of librarianship. Not only did collection development officers and bibliographers select and acquire new resources, they also conducted use and user studies, prepared careful collection policies to guide their work, and they participated in preservation and cooperation to extend the life and scope of collections.

Factors for Change: From Development to Management of Collections

I think three factors were primarily responsible for this evolution from collection development to collection management. First, the constricting budget situation made it impossible to build collections indiscriminately. Librarians were forced to develop and manage scarce resources, with an emphasis on "management." Second, it became clear, or at least clearer, that research and use of library collections was changing. Osburn, for example, presented a persuasive case for the emergence of the sciences in the post-Sputnik period, and their new dominance over the once humanities-centric university. Kent's in-depth study of the use of library material over a seven-year period at the University of Pittsburgh sent shock waves through the scholarly community, even occasioning a faculty investigation of its legitimacy at the University of Pittsburgh. Kent and his research team found "that any given book purchased had only slightly better than one chance in two of ever being borrowed." As books on the shelves aged and did not circulate, their likelihood of ever circulating diminished to as low as one chance in fifty.[4] Better matching library users and their needs to library acquisitions and services became a major interest of the collection management movement.

A third factor that influenced the evolution of collection development and management was the information technology revolution. Librarians were fairly early adopters of new information technology. The creation of online library catalogs and the automation of circulation and technical services began in some libraries in the early 1970s and picked up considerable speed over the next twenty years. By the mid 1980s reference services were adopting online tools, moving from mediated to unmediated services over the next decade. The one holdout (and still the holdout in some pockets of research libraries) was the collections area, which was the last to be affected by this new digital technology. But as scholarly materials moved beyond reference databases and catalogs into full-text journals and e-books in the mid to late 1990s, there was no escaping the significant changes underway. Print, which held sway in the collection development and collection management periods, was still the dominant format in many disciplinary fields in 2000, but digital formats could not be ignored and were quickly being adopted by students, faculty, and librarians. The University of Washington Libraries, for example in Chart 1, found through a survey of their faculty and graduate students that between 1998 and

2001, visits to the physical library were declining while use of networked computers, increasing in offices and homes to access information, was increasing at different rates but still increasing across all the disciplines.[5]

From Collections to Knowledge Management

The evolution of "collection development" to "collection management" to what, at the beginning of the 21st century, I would call "knowledge management" is largely focused for me on the concept and meaning of "collection." A collection, while still vitally important to a research library, is too static and too limited a concept to fully describe the range of information resources now offered to users. As we all know by now, digital information resources offered by our libraries to our users may or may not be actually owned by or housed in our libraries. In a new information universe characterized by multiple and changing formats and by networked access, does the term "collection" really convey what research librarians do today? Are the databases and electronic

CHART 1

Type of Library Use by Group and Academic Area						
University of Washington Library Newsletter Winter 2002						
	Visit in person		*Use office computer*		*Use home computer*	
Faculty	1998	2001	1998	2001	1998	2001
Health Sciences	37.9	28.1	76.2	75.7	40.5	43.4
Humanities/Soc Science	60.7	56.4	70.2	76.7	47.1	51.5
Science/Engineering	49.3	41.8	64.7	75.4	23.6	33.9
All Faculty	47.3	40.6	71.0	76.1	37.4	43
Graduate Students						
Health Sciences	79.7	59.6	39.8	50.6	49.2	59.6
Humanities/Soc Science	82.5	72.1	47.5	56.1	52.0	62.6
Science/Engineering	68.2	45.1	57.4	69.4	32.6	42.5
All Graduate Students	77.7	59.6	48.1	58.5	45.7	55.2

Source: University of Washington Library *Newsletter*, Winter 2002. Used with permission.

texts we lease and the Internet sites we link to really our "collections"? And beyond digital surrogates for print formats–online reference tools, full-text electronic articles, and e-books–do World Wide Web sites, preprint archives, learning objects, and the burgeoning array of unpublished digital assets being created on our campuses qualify as "collections"?

In my own attempt to better define this new situation where the boundaries seemed to be expanding well beyond traditional "collections," I stumbled onto the name "knowledge management." What I meant by this new name was simply that collection management had to be extended to cover more new and emerging forms and arrangements of information resources in the digital age. Little really did I know that "knowledge management" was a new field of information science and business management that was developing a rich literature and practice of its own.

DEFINING AND LEARNING: WHAT IS KNOWLEDGE MANAGEMENT AND HOW CAN IT HELP LIBRARIES?

Data, Information, and Knowledge

One's first encounter with the field of knowledge management is likely to be over discussions and arguments about definition. What is knowledge management? What is knowledge? Can you really manage knowledge? Knowledge management textbooks and introductory articles to the field often begin by describing the distinctions among data, information, and knowledge, although even here at the beginning, the boundaries blur among these broad epistemological categories.

Data are simple, discrete, facts and figures such as names, characteristics, and amounts. Information is a bit more complex, for it organizes data for a meaningful purpose.[6] Data might be a table of circulation statistics, but once those statistics are arranged, charted, annotated, or organized in a meaningful way to describe, say, trends in library use, you have information. Knowledge is much more complex, and a working definition of it that I like was given by Davenport and Prusak in the their book on knowledge management entitled *Working Knowledge*. According to Davenport and Prusak, "Knowledge is a fluid mix of framed experience, values, contextual information, and expert insight that provides a framework for evaluating and incorporating new experience and information. It originates and is applied in the minds of knowers. In organizations, it often becomes embedded not only in documents and repositories but also in organizational routines, processes, practices, and norms."[7] While data and information are in a sense bound objects, knowledge is much more a process, a dynamic, or an ability to understand and to share understanding. We would not hesitate for example to say, "Send me the data you have on circulation for the last year," or "Give me the information you have about how students are using the library." However, we would not say in this same way, "Send me the knowledge you have on circulation for the last year" or "Give me the knowledge you have about how students are using the library." Knowledge, even in common usage, denotes something that is tied to the knower, something not easily given away.[8] How, then, can one manage an intangible, internal asset like knowledge?

Explicit and Tacit and Knowledge

David Blair in his excellent overview article "Knowledge Management: Hype, Hope, or Help?" provides insight into the difference between information management and knowledge management. According to Blair, "Knowledge Management is not so much the management of tangible assets such as data or information, but the active management and support of expertise."[9] Expertise exists in people, and much of this kind of knowledge is tacit rather than explicit. Some of it is expressible; some of it is not. The distinction between tacit (or implicit) and explicit knowledge is another important concept in knowledge management. Chart 2, based on work by Claire McInerney, gives a good example of the characteristics of these two types of knowledge.[10]

Basically, tacit knowledge is personal, or in some cases organizational, and includes skills, heuristics or rules of thumb, habits, culture, undocumented history, and ways of thinking. Tacit knowledge is present in a person or an organization, but it is not written down or documented, and it is often difficult to express or describe. "Explicit knowledge," on the other hand, "is knowledge that has been explained, recorded, or documented."[11] An explicit knowledge artifact, for example, a final report of a project, may embed knowledge in a document, but this is not really knowledge per se by many definitions, since knowledge only really happens "in the minds of knowers." Understanding the importance of expertise and tacit knowledge and understanding the personal, social, and dynamic nature of knowledge underlies many of the strategies of knowledge management.

Social and Dynamic Nature of Knowledge

This is not to say that data and information management are not important, for they are certainly supporting strategies within knowledge management. The ability to capture, share, and preserve data, information, and explicit knowledge are essential to successful knowledge management. This, of course, is the area of endeavor where most information technologists and librarians concentrate their attention: managing information technology hardware, software, and collections of information. But knowledge management really requires a broader perspective, for in addition to data and information management, we must also look to the

CHART 2

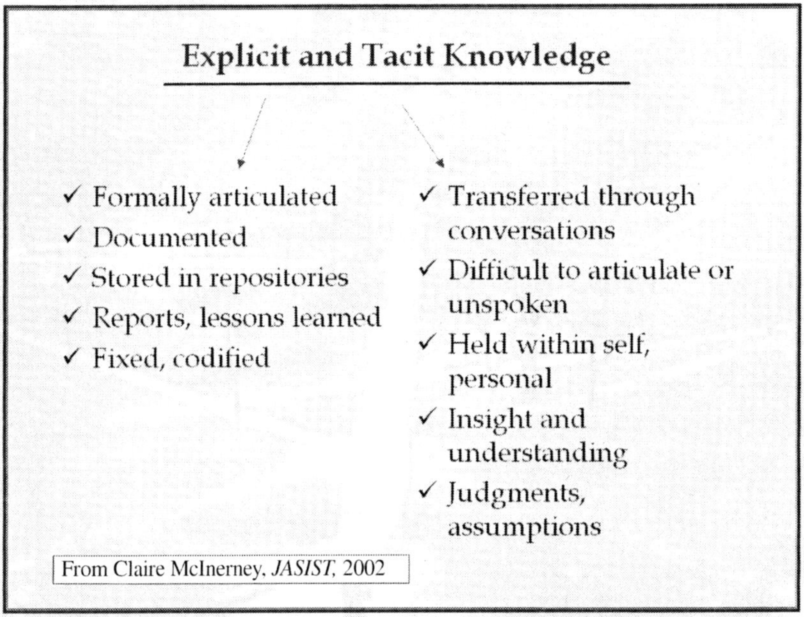

Explicit and Tacit Knowledge

✓ Formally articulated

✓ Documented

✓ Stored in repositories

✓ Reports, lessons learned

✓ Fixed, codified

✓ Transferred through conversations

✓ Difficult to articulate or unspoken

✓ Held within self, personal

✓ Insight and understanding

✓ Judgments, assumptions

From Claire McInerney, *JASIST,* 2002

Adapted from Claire McInerney's "Knowledge Management and the Dynamic Nature of Knowledge," *Journal of the American Society for Information Science and Technology,* 53 (12) 1011.

knowledge workers themselves, to tacit as well as explicit knowledge, and to the social and cultural issues around knowledge creation and sharing. In knowledge management, we are asked to answer questions such as: Are workers encouraged to share knowledge? Is expertise in the organization identified and shared? Can we capture and share more tacit knowledge from individuals and the organization? Who does knowledge, which by its nature is usually a very personal asset, belong to anyhow?

THE KNOWLEDGE BANK PROJECT AT THE OHIO STATE UNIVERSITY

Extending the Expertise of Librarians

We are trying to build an enterprise-wide knowledge management system at the Ohio State University and put into practice some of the guiding concepts of librarianship and knowledge management. From an academic research librarian perspective, the simplest way to describe what we are trying to do is say that we are extending the expertise of librarians to manage all types of information, not just the structured, published information we have traditionally been asked to collect, organize, and preserve. Lorcan Dempsey, Vice President for Research at OCLC, who serves on our Knowledge Bank Planning Team, has graphically described this broader universe of information types in the grid in Chart 3 below.

You can see from this graphical representation that the predominance of cataloging, or what we might today call metadata, as represented in OCLC's WorldCat falls in the upper left quadrant of the graph where structure (formal publication) and lack of uniqueness are high characteristics of the information types. These types include the kinds of published material–books, journals, newspapers, government documents, etc.–that librarians have concentrated on acquiring, cataloging, and preserving. The lower left quadrant, which represents information types of generally high structure and high uniqueness does

CHART 3

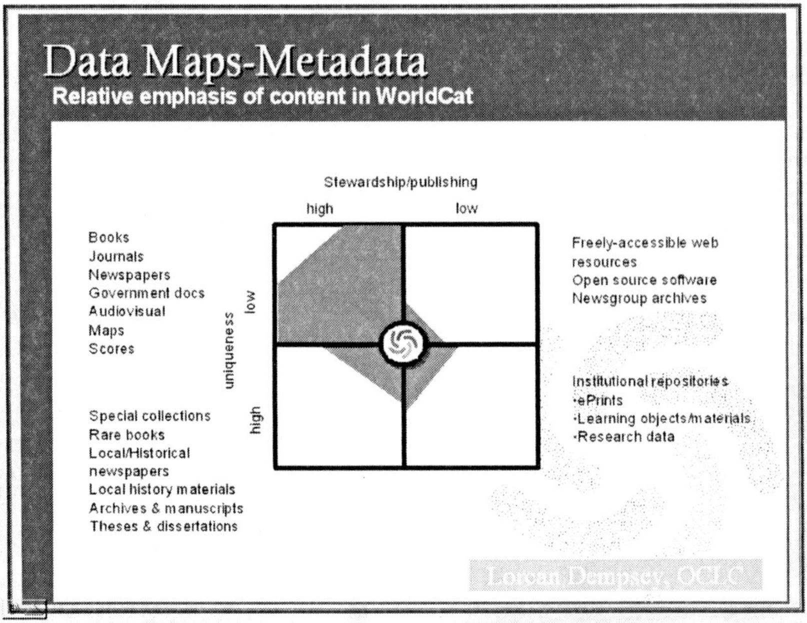

Source: Lorcan Dempsey, Vice President for Research, OCLC. Used with permission.

include some types of information that libraries have paid attention to as well: special collections of rare and valuable books and manuscripts. But beyond these types, libraries have paid little or only limited attention to new information formats and arrangements that are unpublished, unstructured, and unique.

The Genesis of the Knowledge Bank Concept

The Knowledge Bank project at the Ohio State University began in the summer of 2001 when a high-level University task force on distance learning approached me as Director of Libraries with a conceptual model for better managing and using the intellectual digital assets of the institution. They presented me with the following model as seen in Chart 4.

You can see running from left to right in Chart 4 that the model begins with faculty content and ends with a portfolio of learning packages that would be used in distance learning and continuing education programs. For our purposes, the most interesting section of the model is the middle section where something called the "Knowledge Bank" is envisioned. The Knowledge Bank is to be a digital institutional repository–an interdisciplinary, multi-media storehouse of knowledge capital. The task force made up of several university vice presidents and deans came to me with this model because they believed the library should take the lead in creating the Knowledge Bank. If we had the experience and expertise to manage published information, could we not extend this expertise to all of the intellectual assets of the University? What I think is most important to note here about our local story is, first, that this group of senior administrators saw for themselves a growing need to manage the University's digital assets, and second, that they recognized in the library the expertise and experience to lead this effort.

The Knowledge Bank Plan

The Ohio State University Libraries did take up this exciting challenge, and over the course of the next year we developed a plan for creating the Knowledge Bank. We worked closely with faculty and technologists on campus, particularly with the staff of the Chief Information Officer, and we turned to our vibrant community of information services in central Ohio to seek assistance from OhioLINK, OCLC, and Chemical Abstract Services. By the summer of 2002, we had completed our initial plan and shared it with the University.

This plan (see Chart 5 for the cover page of this plan's proposal) and other documentation on the Knowledge Bank project at the Ohio State University are freely available at following web site: http://www.lib.ohio-state.edu/Lib_Info/scholarcom/KbpRroposal.html. Sally Rogers, the OSU Libraries' Assis-

CHART 4

The Knowledge Bank Conceptual Model

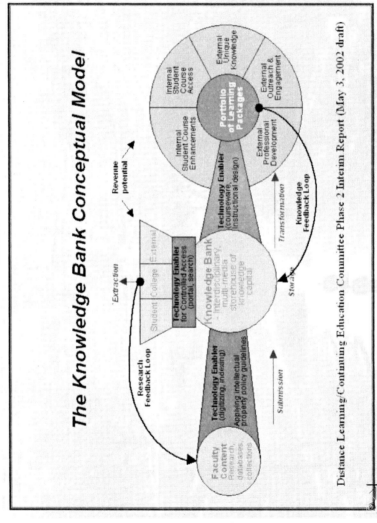

Distance Learning/Continuing Education Committee Phase 2 Interim Report (May 3, 2002 draft)

Source: Ohio State University, Distance Learning/Continuing Education Committee Report, May 3, 2002.

CHART 5

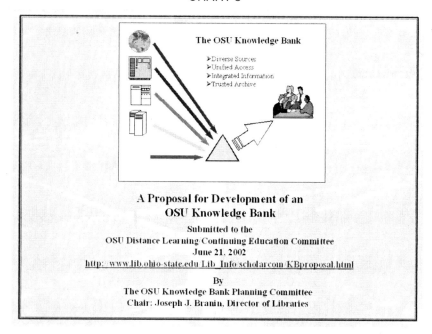

The OSU Knowledge Bank

➢Diverse Sources
➢Unified Access
➢Integrated Information
➢Trusted Archive

**A Proposal for Development of an
OSU Knowledge Bank**

Submitted to the
OSU Distance Learning Continuing Education Committee
June 21, 2002
http://www.lib.ohio-state.edu Lib_Info scholarcom KBproposal.html

By
The OSU Knowledge Bank Planning Committee
Chair: Joseph J. Branin, Director of Libraries

Source: Ohio State University Libraries, A Proposal for Development of an OSU Knowledge Bank, June 21, 2002.

tant Director for Information Technology, has provided much of the leadership for this project, and she has published an article on the Knowledge Bank in the journal *portal: Libraries and the Academy* entitled "Developing an Institutional Knowledge Bank at Ohio State University: From Concept to Action Plan."[12] Since much information is already publicly available about the Knowledge Bank project, I will not review it here in any detail. Instead, I just want to point to some of its key features and end by relating it to the broader professional trend or evolution I see in moving from collection management to knowledge management.

Responding to New Types of Digital Information Assets

Over the last two years, as we have planned and begun to implement the Knowledge Bank project, several important themes have emerged. First, information technology is at a level of maturity now that more and more faculty and students are adapting it not just to access information but also to create new information. On campuses, in departments, in research centers, and among individual faculty and students, there is an explosive growth of digital information assets underway. As we worked on the Knowledge Bank project and started to build an inventory of digital projects at the University, we were amazed at the amount and variety of digital assets being created on campus. Faculty and students are creating databases or collections of digital still and moving images, sound files, and factual files. They are creating learning objects, e-portfolios, electronic theses and dissertations. Many aspects of courses are moving online with the adoption of course management systems. Faculty and students are creating their own web sites to share research and learning. These activities are happening in all of the disciplines across campus, from the individual art undergraduate to research teams working on big science projects.

Second, we soon found that we were not alone in discovering this phenomenon, and that other universities such as MIT, the University of Washington, and the University of California system were working on ways to help their faculty and institutions better manage the rapidly expanding array of intellectual digital assets being produced on their campuses. We were particularly impressed with MIT efforts to create Dspace, an institutional repository platform that could be used to store and preserve all of the new kinds of digital objects being created by their faculty. Not only was MIT developing a tool we thought we might need, but they were doing it in a very open way. All of their planning and technical information were available from their web site at <http://www. dspace.org/>, and the software platform that forms Dspace is built using open source code. We were fortunate to join MIT in a Mellon grant that provides support for the implementation and testing of Dspace for an institutional repository.

A Broad and Evolutionary Approach to Knowledge Management

Third, we spend a great deal of time on definition, scope, and general strategy. What really is the Knowledge Bank and how will we implement it? We decided to take a broad and evolutionary approach to our project. The Knowledge Bank would not just be an institutional repository but instead a much broader enterprise-wide knowledge management system. It would be a "referatory" as well as a "repository," and it would encompass and coordinate a multiplicity of information services at the University. Chart 6 lists the kinds of services and resources the Knowledge Bank would cover.

Our strategy, out of forethought and necessity, has been to address the Knowledge Bank project in a broad, inclusive, and evolutionary manner: inclusive, because we think an institutional repository will not be very successful as an isolated service or tool; and evolutionary, because we believe it will

CHART 6

Digital <u>Knowledge Bank</u> at OSU

➤ Online Published Material
  • E-books, e-journals, government documents, handbooks
➤ Online Reference Tools
  • Catalogs, indexes, dictionaries, encyclopedias, directories
➤ Online Information Services
  • Scholar's portal, alumni portal, chat reference, online tutorials, e-reserves, e-course packs, technology help center
➤ Electronic Records Management
➤ Administrative Data Warehouse
➤ Digital Publishing Assistance
  • Pre-print services
  • E-books, e-journal support
  • Web site development and maintenance

➤ Faculty Research Directory
➤ Digital Institutional Repository
  • Digital special collections
  • Rich media (multimedia)
  • Data sets and files
  • Theses/dissertations
  • Faculty publications, pre-publications, working papers
  • Educational materials
    • Learning objects
    • Course reserves/E-course pack materials
    • Course Web sites
➤ Information Policy
➤ Research/Development in Digital Information Services
  • User needs studies
  • Applying best practice
  • Assistance with Technology Transfer

Source: Ohio State University Libraries, A Proposal for Development of an OSU Knowledge Bank, June 21, 2002.

take time and money, which is in short supply these days, to change and add to the organization of information services in any university. The Knowledge Bank project is not a short-term project, but one that will likely be underway for five to ten years before it is mainstreamed or institutionalized at the University.

Librarians as Knowledge Managers

Fourth, while digital technology is pushing and allowing for new information services and products, the adoption of new approaches and organization has always depended very much on working out basic personal and social issues. Our Knowledge Bank project is paying close attention to issues related to faculty and student involvement, motivation, and buy-in. We are also encouraging librarians and technologist on campus to work together to create new service models–ones that will emphasize outreach, consultation, and training.

If we as librarians are to extend our expertise in selecting, organizing, and preserving information to new forms of less formal, unpublished material, we must be willing to get outside the routines and the walls of the traditional library and work more directly with technologists, faculty, and students.

And this brings me to my closing point. Who is more central to this effort than the subject specialist or the bibliographer in a research library? Several years ago Patricia Battin (my mentor in 1986 when I was Council on Library Resources Intern at Columbia University) and Brian Hawkins made the following observation, "Librarians can no longer meet the information needs of faculty and students through the traditional avenue of simply adding to their collections."[13] I agree: librarians must extend their expertise beyond collection management to knowledge management. At the Ohio State University Libraries our subject specialists are building the inventory of digital resources and services on campus, and they are creating the relationships that allow the librarians and the faculty to work more closely with each other in creating managing, sharing, and preserving a wider range of digital assets. For example, James Bracken, our Assistant Director for Research and the Bibliographer for English Literature, is working with Steven Acker, a Journalism Professor and Technologist, to design a system for the creation and preservation of learning objects. They have collaborated on a graduate course on learning objects (see the course description in Chart 7) that has advanced our understanding and our procedures for dealing with this new kind of digital asset.

I think all of us as academic librarians, whether we work in administration, collection management, reference, or technical services, must take on new roles as knowledge managers. In this new role we will be

- *Knowledge management developers*, working more closely with faculty and students to design, organize, and maintain a broader range of digital assets;
- *Knowledge management integrators*, having a more active role in the educational and research mission of the university, integrating information resources and services in course and research projects;
- *Knowledge management educators*, teaching and training students and faculty in information literacy and how to organize, preserve, and share their own information resources;
- *Knowledge management researchers*, applying library and information science and new digital technology to create new organizational (metadata), retrieval, and storage (preservation) options.

CHART 7

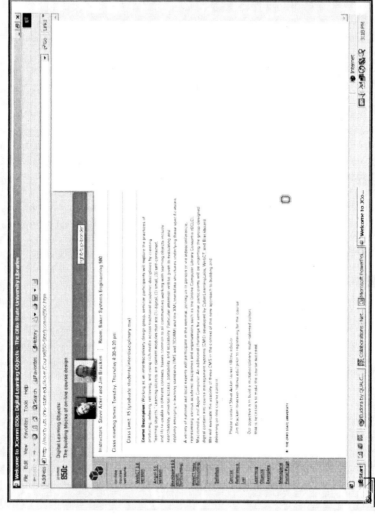

Source: Ohio State University Course Web Page, 2002.

REFERENCES

1. Branin, Joseph et al. 2000. "The Changing Nature of Collection Management in Research Libraries." *Library Resources & Technical Services* 44: 23-32.

2. Perkins, David L., ed. 1979. *Guidelines For Collection Development*. Chicago: American Library Association. Osburn, Charles B. 1979. *Academic Research and Library Resources: Changing Pattern in America*. Westport, Conn.: Greenwood Press. Kent, Allen et al. 1979. *Use of Library Materials: The University of Pittsburgh study*. New York: Marcel Dekker.

3. Mosher, Paul H. 1981. "Fighting back: From collection development to collection management." Unpublished address given at the Collection Management and Development Institute, Stanford University, July 6-10. Stanford, Calif.

4. Kent, 10.

5. University of Washington Libraries *Newsletter*. 2002.

6. Drucker, Peter. (1998). "The Coming of the New Organization." *Harvard Business Review on Knowledge Management*. Cambridge, MA: Harvard Business School Press.

7. Davenport, Thomas H. & Prusak, Laurence. (1998). *Working Knowledge: How Organizations Manage What They Know*. Boston: Harvard Business School Press, 5.

8. Blair, David C. (2002). "Knowledge Management: Hype, Hope, or Help?" *Journal of the American Society for Information Science and Technology*. 53 (12): 1019-1028.

9. Blair, 1020.

10. McInerney, Claire. (2002). "Knowledge Management and the Dynamic Nature of Knowledge." *Journal of the American Society for Information Science and Technology*, 53 (12): 1009-1018.

11. McInerney, 1012.

12. Rogers, Sally A. (2003) "Developing an Institutional Knowledge Bank at Ohio State University: From Concept to Action Plan." *portal: Libraries and the Academy*, 3 (1): 125-136.

13. Hawkins, Brian L. & Battin, Patricia, eds. 1998. *The Mirage of Continuity: Reconfiguring Academic Information Resources for the 21st Century*. Washington, D.C.: Council on Library and Information Resources and Association of American Universities, 7.

Portals, Access, and Research Libraries

Mary E. Jackson

INTRODUCTION

It is an honor to be asked to participate in the University of Oklahoma Libraries Conference again this year. I would like to thank Dean Lee and his colleagues for hosting yet another in a long line of successful conferences.

Those of you who attended last year's conference will recall that I described the Scholars Portal Project.[1] I stopped short of announcing the vendor selected by the project participants as the conference was held two weeks before the selection was made public. For those who weren't here last year, I will provide a very brief background on the project. The main portion of my talk will describe the current status of the project. I will also summarize other ARL portal-related activities, specifically the update on the survey of portal applications in ARL member institutions.

The Scholars Portal Project has evolved out of a series of conversations over the past three years. Attendees at the 1999 Association of Research Libraries (ARL)-OCLC Strategic Issues Forum first articulated the concern that libraries were in danger of abandoning their constituencies to the commercial information services in the web environment. Students and even some faculty were using and appear to prefer Google and other commercial search engines over the library's online catalog, in large part because of the user-friendly interface and ease of use. What would research libraries need to do to ensure that

Mary E. Jackson is Director of Collections and Access Programs, Association of Research Libraries, Washington, DC (E-mail: mary@arl.org). © 2003 Mary E. Jackson. Printed with permission.

[Haworth co-indexing entry note]: "Portals, Access, and Research Libraries." Jackson, Mary E. Co-published simultaneously in *Journal of Library Administration* (The Haworth Information Press, an imprint of The Haworth Press, Inc.) Vol. 39. No. 4, 2003, pp. 57-63; and: *Improved Access to Information: Portals, Content Selection, and Digital Information* (ed: Sul H. Lee) The Haworth Information Press, an imprint of The Haworth Press, Inc., 2003, pp. 57-63. Single or multiple copies of this article are available for a fee from The Haworth Document Delivery Service [1-800-HAWORTH, 9:00 a.m. - 5:00 p.m. (EST). E-mail address: docdelivery@haworthpress.com].

http://www.haworthpress.com/web/JLA
Digital Object Identifier: 10.1300/J111v39n04_06

students and scholars were able to use fine quality and library-vetted information that has been a cornerstone of research library collections?

Jerry Campbell, Chief Information Officer and Dean of University Libraries, University of Southern California, built on the discussions at the Forum in his white paper, "The Case for Creating a Scholars Portal to the Web: A White Paper."[2] He coined the phrase Scholars Portal. He asserted that the Scholars Portal should include high-quality content, be based on standards, search across a range of databases, offer a variety of supporting tools, offer enhanced services such a digital reference, and integrate electronic thesauri. Campbell also offered some strategies to address the growing problem. He suggested that ARL seriously pursue the feasibility of developing a "library.org" web presence and argued for a collaborative partnership approach.

With the need clearly articulated, ARL established the ARL Scholars Portal Working Group in early 2001 to develop strategies for pursing the concept of a "library.org" presence on the Web. The working group, chaired by Campbell, recommended the construction of a suite of web-based services that would connect the higher education community as directly as possible with quality information resources that contribute to the teaching and learning process and that advance research. The working group decided that the first focus should be on the development of specifications (conceptual, functional, and technical) for a "super discovery tool." This discovery tool will enable a user to search across certain limited but diverse and distributed websites, library catalogs, and databases of information resources to retrieve and integrate the results in a single presentation. The working group envisioned the search results to be a merged list of citations, de-duplicated, with indicators of the sources from which the search engine identified the citation. The list will be capable of being sorted, for example, to reflect whether the items are available immediately as full text, available in the local library collection, or via ILL or another delivery option.

The discovery tool needs to be more than a sophisticated search tool, as it will also link need to other library services. Users are expected to rely on a variety of access and delivery mechanisms, including linking directly to full-text articles, digitized resources and recommended websites, retrieving print materials from the library shelves, or requesting document delivery of non-locally held materials through interlibrary loan or commercial vendors. Users will also link to 24/7 reference services to consult with a reference librarian.

Recognizing that it was neither necessary nor particularly desirable that ARL develop the discovery tool itself, the working group conducted an environmental scan in the spring of 2001 to identify potential partners (commercial and otherwise) with whom to collaborate in the tool's development. The working group did not limit its collaboration to a single partner, but with the support of the ARL Board of Directors, entered into an agreement with Fretwell-Downing, Inc. (FD).

SCHOLARS PORTAL PROJECT LAUNCHED

On May 1, 2002 ARL announced the launch of the Scholars Portal Project,[3] a collaborative effort between several ARL member libraries and Fretwell-Downing Inc. (FD). The Scholars Portal Project seeks to demonstrate the viability of the vision articulated by the working group with one vendor's products. The ARL Scholars Portal Working Group selected FD to participate in the three-year project after making an assessment of portal software tools available in the marketplace, how close the tools come to fulfilling and sustaining the Scholars Portal vision, and the readiness and experience of the companies to collaborate on advancing priority enhancements. The initiative is also intended to encourage other vendors to enter the marketplace with competitive tools or expand existing products to advance portal functionality.

The initial libraries participating in the project include the University of Southern California, University of California–San Diego, Dartmouth College, University of Arizona, Arizona State University, Iowa State University, and the University of Utah.

FD products included in the three-year project include ZPORTAL, Z2Web, Z'MBOL, and OL2. The initial focus will be on deploying ZPORTAL to deliver cross-domain searching of licensed and openly available content in a range of subject fields and from multiple institutions. The portal will aggregate and integrate the results of the search, and support delivery of the content to the user. Future phases of the project will add other services to the portal that improve user access to and use of information resources. For example, enhancements include integration of the searching tool within the local online learning environment for a course, and linkage to a 24/7 digital reference service to consult with a reference librarian.

The initial participants in the Project and FD will collaborate to develop additional functionality they identify as critical and, with input from the teaching faculty, will refine, develop, and evaluate the capabilities provided by the portal in teaching and library production environments. It is anticipated that in most academic environments, the tools developed through the Scholars Portal Project will function as a library channel within a university-wide portal. ARL's role is to manage the project. ARL will also continue to monitor available tools and products and report on the experiences to the library community.

CURRENT STATE OF THE PROJECT

During the second half of 2002, FD installed software in all sites and trained teams of staff at each institution. The project is designed to enable each site to run the software locally, customize the user interface, use local authentication services, and add content appropriate to and needed by their communities. Each site is also defining its target audience. Iowa State University is aiming the portal at the entire campus, the University of Utah is focused on a specific department, and the University of California–San Diego is targeting a specific user group. Some have redefined their initial target audience to more closely match the content that is already available. All participants are taking a very pragmatic approach to this project.

Each institution appointed a local project manager and those individuals established an Implementers Group in early 2003. A project web site has been established, meetings have been held, and regular conference calls and online discussion lists facilitate communication among the project managers and their colleagues.

In early 2003 two of the seven participants have introduced the software to their user populations. Iowa State University calls their portal "Find It!" and it is available from the library's home page.[4] The University of Arizona's *Beta-SEARCH* is displayed alongside the library's "classic" multi-search system. *Beta-SEARCH* is described as a "prototype interface" and "work in progress."[5] The other participants have expressed similar plans to bring up the software by the end of calendar year 2003 and undertake limited promotion or marketing at the onset. Participants are concerned that users will not embrace the portal if it does not include content specific and in sufficient variety to their area of research or interest.

FOCUSING ON CONTENT

One of the anticipated benefits of a collaborative project was that participants could share their work on linking to public web sites or licensed electronic resources. It was anticipated that research libraries would have significant overlap in the content they would make available through their portals. This collaborative project offers the potential to eliminate the growing duplication of effort in maintaining links to the same web site or to the same licensed electronic resources by multiple institutions. Like other portal products, FD's software requires a script be written for each web resource, and configuration be completed for each resource searchable via Z39.50. In an effort to begin narrowing the content each participant wanted to include in the portal, the project managers, in collaboration with local collection development managers, identified their "top" web sites.

Over 130 different web sites were identified, and the overlap was not what participants had expected. Only two web sites were identified by six of the seven participants; five sites were selected by three of the seven participants; and 21 were selected by only two of the seven. A total of 105 web sites were selected by only one participant, which meant that 80% of the web sites in this initial list were unique to a single institution. Examples of the sites on the participants lists include: PubMed, SciFinderScholar, Bibliography of Native North American Studies, GeoRef, Latin American Weekly Report, and StatUSA. These initial lists do not represent the universe of what the participants want to include in a fully functioning portal. The challenge to develop scripts for all the web sites the participants wanted to have searchable via ZPORTAL in a time-frame acceptable to the participants dictated that a different approach would be required.

Project managers decided that a subject approach to web sites might increase the overlap. A total of nine subject areas were identified: biomedical, engineering, environmental sciences, full-text/"panic," general reference, history, literary criticism, nursing, and social sciences. Project managers were asked to list web sites for these subjects. A total of 227 web sites were identified, with 198 sites appearing on only one subject list, or 87% unique. After reviewing the overlap among the lists and voting on which were their "top" subject lists, project managers agreed to begin with literature, full-text/"panic," and environmental studies. The full-text/ "panic" is aimed at the undergraduate student with a paper due in hours and need only content available in full-text.

The selection of Z39.50 targets is following a similar process of narrowing down the resources that need to be added first. It's difficult to determine what needs to be added first; project managers want to include as much content in their local implementations as their users want and need. The challenge of adding Z39.50 or web content quickly is not unique to ZPORTAL; other research libraries have voiced concern about the time-consuming nature of adding resources to other portal products.

ARL SURVEY ON PORTAL IMPLEMENTATIONS

The Scholars Portal Project is not the only portal-related initiative among the ARL member institutions. In an effort to monitor other initiatives, ARL conducted a survey of its members in the spring of 2002 to identify the state of current or planned research library applications of portals that have certain characteristics or functions. For the purpose of that survey, a portal was defined as a tool that includes a search engine that offered the user the capability to search across multiple sources and integrate the results of those searches (a single search function), and that includes at least one kind of supporting service for the user (such as requesting retrieval or delivery of non-digital material, online reference help, etc.).[6]

A total of 77 ARL member libraries responded; 16 of the 19 positive responses were "close enough" to the definition to be included in the final analysis. Thirteen of the 16 had developed their portals locally, perhaps evolving from the library's web page. All were aimed at the general university community. Fifteen of the 16 offer online reference help. Half offered customization, seven included push features, 13 portals were able to limit searches and ten sorted results. Seven eliminated duplicates. Nearly all, 14 of the 16, surveyed their users, and 11 of them used focus groups.

All respondents listed additional features they would like to include in their portals. These features include: additional customization, navigation by subject, more personalization, customized links to individual journal titles, and the ability to offer alumni access to licensed resources.

Recognizing that many ARL member institutions are actively investigating and implementing portals since the survey was conducted nearly a year ago, ARL's Portal Applications Working Group polled ARL members in December 2002 to update the snapshot of portal activity. Given the variant definitions and characterizations of portals, ARL asked four questions:

1. Does your library provide cross-resource searching?
2. Does your portal or web site permit customized data mining of content or metadata?
3. Does your web page permit users to personalize searches, screens, or features?
4. Do you offer any supporting services such as a link to interlibrary loan or online reference?

The following findings are preliminary, but are being shared with you to show the range of answers and responses. The final results will be published by ARL later this year. A total of 34 libraries responded to the questions. Of the 34, 24 offered cross-resource searching. However, some of the comments suggest that not all offer cross-resource searching. One indicated that they offer cross-resource searching only within one resource. A second responded that they offer it, with qualification. And, a third responded "sort of." Several indicated that it is under development or they are exploring the Open URL. So, it is likely that fewer than 24 actually offer cross-resource searching.

Only six of the 34 respondents offer data mining. Several indicated that this feature was in a future release of the products they were using. Only six of the 34 permit users to personalize their web pages.

The responses to the fourth question suggest that many web sites have incorporated one or more supporting services that are also found in portals. A total of 29 indicated that they offer one or more supporting services. Twelve of the 29 support online or virtual reference, 13 feature ILL forms, 3 permit links to electronic reserve systems, and one responded they offer "online virtual services" without explaining what is meant by that phrase.

The members of the Portal Applications Working Group are in the process of conducting follow-up interviews with the directors of the institutions that responded. The conversations are designed to add additional context to the responses. ARL will synthesize the findings and publish the results later this spring.

I would like to conclude with two quotes from the initial survey responses. The following vision statements included in the responses signify the fluid and localized nature of the definition of a portal.

> *A campus source of first resort for faculty, students, staff directly or remotely. Critical value-added feature is the full integration of enterprise systems, behind the scenes, and addition of rich content drawn from those systems or from databases or licensed content.*

> *A gateway that offers selected library resources, both subscribed and non-subscribed, enhances discovery of information, and provides tools and guidance in the use of this information, all to strengthen learning and research.*

CONCLUSION

The Scholars Project and similar portal initiatives in other ARL member institutions will be characterized as successful if users can discover a wide range of content; capture that content using harvesting and/or delivery tools; manipulate text using text-processing and citation management tools; distribute content by the use of contribution and publication tools; and consult by means of access to virtual reference services and electronic scholarly communities.

Thank you for your attention. I welcome your questions.

NOTES

1. Mary E. Jackson, "The ARL Scholars Portal Initiative," *Journal of Library Administration* 36, no. 3, 2002, pp. 81-91.

2. Jerry Campbell, "The Case for Creating a Scholars Portal to the Web: A White Paper," http://www.arl.org/newsltr/211/portal.html.

3. "Seven ARL Libraries Launch Scholars Portal Project in Collaboration with Fretwell-Downing, Inc." http://www.arl.org/arl/pr/scholars_portal.html.

4. Iowa State University Libraries' home page: http://www.lib.iastate.edu/.

5. University of Arizona Libraries' home page: http://dizzy.library.arizona.edu/multisearch.shtml.

6. Karen A. Wetzel and Mary E. Jackson, "Portal Functionality Provided by ARL Libraries: Results of an ARL Survey," http://www.arl.org/newsltr/222/portalsurvey.html.

Selectors, Subject Knowledge, and Digital Collections

Edward Shreeves

In an article titled "Twilight of the Gods: Bibliographers in the Electronic Age," Dan Hazen speculates about the role of bibliographers–a term I'll take to mean collection management librarians with some degree of subject expertise–in the emerging information environment (Hazen, 2000). He alludes to the "golden age" of collection development, when collections–collections in print–were king, and bibliographers could be nearly as important as directors, at least in the eyes of faculty. In the early twenty-first century, collections are no longer king, except perhaps to some of our humanities faculty, and the bibliographer/subject specialist model of collection development has been in decline, or at least transition, for some time. If the notion of the collection-centered library was not done in by the misleading rhetoric of the access vs. ownership battle, it has been overwhelmed by the information explosion, Elsevier and company, and the chaos of the Web. And yet, if collections and those who build them no longer hold sway, I do sometimes hear the catch-phrase "content is king" in discussions of digital libraries, an allusion to the sense that in the electronic environment, as elsewhere, our users want access to information that is meaningful, accessible and useful–information that allows them to create new knowledge.

I began by thinking about the relationship between portals–one of the announced topics of this conference–and collection development, in particular, the

Edward Shreeves is Associate Director, University of Iowa Libraries, Iowa City, IA (E-mail: edward-shreeves@uiowa.edu).

[Haworth co-indexing entry note]: "Selectors, Subject Knowledge, and Digital Collections." Shreeves, Edward. Co-published simultaneously in *Journal of Library Administration* (The Haworth Information Press, an imprint of The Haworth Press, Inc.) Vol. 39, No. 4, 2003, pp. 65-78; and: *Improved Access to Information: Portals, Content Selection, and Digital Information* (ed: Sul H. Lee) The Haworth Information Press, an imprint of The Haworth Press, Inc., 2003, pp. 65-78. Single or multiple copies of this article are available for a fee from The Haworth Document Delivery Service [1-800-HAWORTH, 9:00 a.m. - 5:00 p.m. (EST). E-mail address: docdelivery@haworthpress.com].

http://www.haworthpress.com/web/JLA
© 2003 by The Haworth Press, Inc. All rights reserved.
Digital Object Identifier: 10.1300/J111v39n04_07

work and skills of collection development librarians. If portals currently seem to offer one of the best ways to help our users find and exploit good content–"good" meaning the content that best meets their information needs–what, if any, is the role of the collection or subject specialist in making portals work? On further consideration, I thought it might be useful to frame the question more broadly, in terms of the relationship between the activities, skills and expertise associated with bibliographers and the evolution of the work of collection development in the digital age. First, a note on vocabulary, which can lead to misunderstandings in this arena. I use the term collection management or development librarian, bibliographer, and selector somewhat interchangeably. I recognize that distinctions could be drawn in terms of functions performed, organizational home, library size, and subject matter covered, and a little later will focus a bit on these distinctions. Second, I use the term collection development to mean those identification and selection activities directed toward the universe of information in all formats and resulting in our user communities gaining access to a defined subset of those resources. I am emphatically not using it to refer only to what we physically acquire and place on our shelves–the artifactual collection.

In a post-modern environment it seems an obvious truism that we view and make sense of the world from the experiences peculiar to our own history. For me, those experiences include nearly a decade as a bibliographer at the UCLA library at the tail end of Hazen's "golden age," if not at the beginning of its transition to what followed, whatever it might be called. I left UCLA to become an administrator for collection development and management (even though the term "information resources" is now part of the title). These influences together have conditioned me to look for, if not to find, the value and importance of subject expertise and collection development skills for almost any environment, including the creation and deployment of portals. Add to this conditioning what Martin Dillon refers to as our natural instinct for survival and self-perpetuation, something that leads us to adhere "with irrational great strength to the patterns" of our job (Dillon, 2002, 329). I hope, however, that I am enough of a skeptic to resist these solipsistic temptations. The remarks that follow reflect thoughts on these issues in response to some recent attempts by Wendy Lougee and others to redefine collection development in the electronic age, and my particular focus is on the potential roles of the selector and the skills that such specialists typically bring to the table.

BIBLIOGRAPHERS AND THE DIGITAL FUTURE

Hazen, in "Twilight of the Gods," reviews the various contexts within which bibliographers have done and continue to do their work. He speculates about the roles they might play in the current hybrid environment, one in which digital information is clearly where the action is. These contexts include the system of scholarly communication, the information marketplace, the academic institutions in which we operate, cooperative programs, and communities of peers, among others. Within these contexts bibliographers "offer subject knowledge, often tied to language skills; familiarity with a system of scholarly communication; and mastery of the associated information marketplace(s)" (Hazen 2000, 838). To these skills we might add considerable familiarity with the local scholarly enterprise, the specific research agendas of faculty, the disciplinary landscape, and often some degree of insight into the local political scene from a faculty, as well as a library, perspective. In the emerging environment Hazen identifies a number of areas where the expertise of bibliographers can make a contribution, and he notes in particular three: the continued building of print, non-print and "owned" electronic collections; the provision of high levels of reference service; and certain types of cooperative activities.

Two features of the landscape mentioned by Hazen offer a potentially fruitful role for the subject specialist. One is the increasing reliance of researchers, especially in the humanities, on an ever-expanding range of resources, in all formats, and often in genres not traditionally collected (try a search on titles "Reading the . . ." in your local catalog). The other feature, arising directly from the non-traditional nature of these resources, is their range, complexity, and impermanence. Certainly general reference librarians often fulfill the role of aide and navigator in this shifting landscape. But research needs, language barriers and cultural issues can move quickly toward greater complexity and obscurity. In these circumstances the subject specialist also needs to play an important role as guide and advisor. Of course, in some measure, the information challenge described here is one that portals and knowledge management systems could help address. I might argue that to the extent they are addressed effectively, the knowledge of content experts will be required. And to the degree that portals and similar systems fall short, these same experts may need to be around to pick up where the software leaves off.

In the early 1990s the University of Iowa Libraries, like many others, wrote a collection development policy for electronic resources. Among other goals, the policy aimed to assert to the campus a central role for the libraries in acquiring and making accessible electronic information resources. It also asserted the role of collection management librarians in selecting these resources–this in an environment where that role was still somewhat in question. We recently reviewed and updated all of our library policies. The review group from our collection advisory committee recommended scrapping the e-resources policy as an independent statement, and incorporating its key concepts into the general collection policy. We accomplished this by adding just a few phrases here and there to that policy, in recognition that roles we had asserted for both the library on the campus stage and selectors on the library stage, were no longer in serious doubt–at least for commercially produced, licensed resources.

One of the arguments of our electronic resources policy document affirmed that electronic resources were simply another format among the many others that libraries "collected." It held that the fundamental criteria on which selection was based did not differ materially from print and those of other formats. We recognized, of course, that there were a host of added considerations the digital medium required us to take into account–everything from user interface to data format to hardware requirements. While so-called traditional formats traveled familiar paths from selection to availability, digital resources demanded new processes, new skills and new protocols to become usable. To some extent, the argument of collection development–that these resources simply reflected another format, subject to the same judgments as any other–is misleading if not disingenuous, at least in practice. The explosion of digital information in both society at large and the academy has been far too pervasive and transformative for us to think of it as just another format. The added demands of the digital medium are certainly not trivial. They have placed much heavier burdens on our organizations, the expertise of our staffs, and our equipment budgets than any other format taken into libraries over the last half century. In addition, the decision-making process for electronic resources has, to a high degree, become centralized and collaborative, quite different from the typically autonomous decision-making exercised by the individual selector. So, while we can assert that the role of the selector is identical or similar for traditional and electronic resources, in fact this is only partially true, and masks a much more complicated situation.

STEWARDSHIP AND FEDERATION

In a recent publication, Wendy Lougee contrasts the traditional practice of collection development, which she terms the full stewardship model, with an alternative she refers to as the federated model (Lougee 2002). The full stewardship model–classical collection development–saw libraries purchase materials, organize them, typically by cataloging, make them available for users, and preserve them for future users. As she notes, most libraries are seeking to apply this model to digital content, with mixed success. All of the four elements of the stewardship model–selection/purchase, organization, availability and preservation–differ significantly in the online environment, although it might be argued that selection–if we separate it from acquisitions–varies the least. Up to a point, at least, the application of subject knowledge, both of the field of study and the publications universe, and an understanding of the user community and its needs, works to inform the selection process in similar ways for traditional and electronic formats. In both the print and digital realm, the application of this knowledge leads to discrimination among alternative ways to spend a finite budget, and results in a decision to purchase a particular set of resources from a much larger universe.

It may be worth a brief detour here to consider the issue of the budget and marketplace. Traditional selection is an expensive proposition. I am not referring solely to the cost of journals and other things bought by the acquisitions budget, but to the cost of time. Some of the earliest forms of library outsourcing are the approval plans that many academic libraries use, in part at least, to reduce the high cost of selection. In the digital preservation arena, some have suggested that it may be more sustainable to save everything than to select only certain things to save, because of the prohibitively high cost of selection. Is this argument extensible to the building of electronic collections, that is, to the process of making decisions about what users will have access to? Can we, as has also been suggested, get out of our users' way, and let them select what they need from the information universe? At least in the short term, the answer would appear to be, probably not. The information resources needed for scholarly work, the products of scholarly communication and much of the primary material on which it is based, are likely to remain scarce commodities, with access limited by licenses and high prices. The promise of institutional repositories, SPARC, the Budapest Initiative and Biomed Central may someday be realized, but the struggle is apt to be protracted, and these low-cost alternative systems of scholarly communication seem likely to coexist with the more familiar high-cost models for some time to come. As long as the budget remains an essential tool for achieving access, whether to traditional or digital resources, a selection decision by library staff will be required to determine which resources we privilege, and which we leave inaccessible, or at least less conveniently accessible, to our users.

This assertion about the similarity of selection in the traditional and digital environment is most true, perhaps, of digital content which the library acquires (and owns) and makes available through servers located on its own campus. But I would argue that it holds true for content delivered from publishers' or aggregators' servers whenever libraries maintain some form of ownership of that data. [I suspect that the "perpetual access" and ownership rights that publishers like Elsevier often include in their contracts are in some measure convenient fictions we use to convince ourselves that the old ownership, or stewardship, model still works in the digital age. Nevertheless, it does drive a number of assumptions guiding decisions about collection development.] It could even be argued that as far as the selection decision-making process goes, the criteria remain largely the same even for those resources which we explicitly lease and have access to only during a limited subscription period. While we own nothing through our Lexis-Nexis contracts, the possibility of this content becoming unavailable seems remote and unlikely, even in difficult economic times. Ownership of electronic resources seems clearly to affect collection decisions in only one area, when we are determining whether to let go of print when both print and electronic versions of a resource are available. But in practice the tremendous uncertainties of digital preservation thwart our ability to make useful distinctions between nominal ownership and leasing of information. This is not to minimize the fundamental importance of this distinction in principle–I assume we all try to negotiate permanent or archival access to any product we license. But in day-to-day practice the difference often fades away.

Lougee goes on to describe an emerging model of collection development that she calls "collection federation." This model is based on several relevant characteristics of our current highly distributed environment. In this environment libraries offer access to content they neither own nor manage, bringing together distributed information sources and making them appear to the user to be an integrated collection. As described by Lougee, the owner/managers of this federated content retain control over their own collections, while the library (or some other agency) makes it available under this federated system. As she notes, such a model implies a more complex role for the library than the full stewardship approach, since the library must balance "distributed content and collection-specific functionality with cross-collection functionality and tools" (Lougee 2002, 6). Even in this model a role remains for some of the skills of traditional collection development. The first step in the process is identification of content and its evaluation by the federating agent, that is, the library. But, while the fundamental intellectual activity remains the same–namely, appraisal of subject content according to certain quality criteria and utility to a given community–the tasks and processes arising from that act of judgment differ fundamentally. Lougee describes the series of actions that might ensue from identification and evaluation. They include negotiation and persuasion, contractual agreements, database analysis and metadata creation, user assessment and task analysis to inform design, development of system architecture, and continuous assessment of functionality, not to mention maintenance of the relationships with content providers. Of course, the selection decision to buy a particular book also sets in motion a number of sometimes complex operations. But long experience and the development of time-tested conventions have made these operations routine, and their complexity seems modest in comparison to the demands of an online federated environment.

One of the greatest organizational challenges, as Lougee notes, is the need for libraries to bring together in functional ways the combination of expertise "relating to the subject domain, content characteristics, access, service and technology. One could add to the list skills related to human-computer interaction, interface design, and usability assessment." By implication, the organizational demands, requiring existing staff to develop expertise in new arenas and to function in new ways, may be far more daunting than the technological. Our existing organizations are still largely designed and staffed to manage the processes associated with a full stewardship model, and not so well adapted to a federated approach. Ironically, some of the skills of the subject specialist may carry over into this environment more readily than those of some other staff. The challenge may lie more in shifting the world view of the selector from the certainties of artifactual ownership to the ambiguities of shifting partnerships and uncertain results that characterize a federated model. Many skills typical of the bibliographer in the stewardship model–the ability to keep up with the literature of a field, and to identify that part of it valuable to local users–can be exercised in relatively autonomous fashion. This is not to say that such autonomy is necessarily desirable (I would argue the opposite), merely that it is not uncommon. In the federated model the ability to work effectively in multifunctional groupings, often outside the library itself, and to achieve goals through influence and persuasion, becomes critical.

"COLLECTIONS AND ACCESS FOR THE 21ST CENTURY SCHOLAR"

In October, 2001 the Association of Research Libraries (ARL) sponsored a forum in Washington, DC on "Collections and Access for the 21st Century Scholar." After the forum a task force was formed to follow up on the discussions and identify agendas for ARL relating to the topic. The December 2002 issue of the ARL newsletter is devoted to their work, and outlines some of the emerging trends in collection management and access strategies among research libraries (ARL 2002). It may be worthwhile to look at some of their findings and observations as yet another indicator of future roles for collection development librarians. In answering the question, "What new approaches are research libraries taking?" the Task Force identified first the expansion of electronic resources and redefinition of collections. They observe that over the last ten years spending on electronic resources has grown from 4% to 16% of members' materials budgets. [It is instructive to remember the corollary, that 84% of members' budgets are still spent on print and other non-electronic formats. Of course, this percentage is probably skewed by the effects of consortial spending, and inconsistencies in the way we account for combination print/electronic materials.] They differentiate the "orderly" processes for acquiring print, and the chaotic processes for selecting and managing electronic resources. They also allude to the use of the budget as a tool to influence the direction of the scholarly communication system, as libraries invest in publishing initiatives that may help solve the problem of high journal prices. In addition, the Task Force reports, libraries are digitizing materials from their own collections, and working with others to publish digital material–akin to the kind of activity Lougee calls collection federation. And in a related development, libraries are assuming responsibility for digital collections outside of their domain, as in the development of institution-wide knowledge management systems, or institutional repositories.

Collections need no longer be defined as "things owned," but rather as the "information resources for which the library invests financial resources–directly and indirectly–to manage, service, or preserve on behalf of library users, regardless of the location of content" (ARL 2002, 13).

Reviewing these "new approaches" or emerging directions for collections and access we encounter a number of themes familiar from the discussions of Lougee and Hazen. Also familiar is the correlation between some of these new directions and the skill sets of bibliographers. Among the most obvious, as expected, is the application of subject and disciplinary knowledge to the selection of electronic resources, and to the selection of collections to digitize. Also recognizable from Lougee's arguments is the role of subject expertise in identifying external digital collections in the selector's spheres of interest and in engineering a productive relationship with their creators or keepers. Somewhat less familiar, but not unimportant, is the implied function of the library to somehow provide a connection to information beyond local control–the vast landscape of the Web. In an article commissioned by the Task Force, Paul Conway notes that libraries need to resolve the tensions between "the Web that we access and the digital content that we provide." He goes on to note that "libraries are being asked or expected to step up to the challenge of acquiring, organizing, and protecting digital content that they have neither created themselves . . . nor licensed from publishers" (Conway 2002, 3).

KNOWLEDGE MANAGEMENT

The report of the ARL task force brings into play another concept that has gained increasing currency, namely knowledge management. Knowledge management is sometimes seen as the natural, or desirable evolution of collection management, which itself emerges from the ideas and practices of collection development. I would call your attention in particular to the discussion of Branin, Groen and Thorin entitled "The Changing Nature of Collection Management in Research Libraries" (Branin 2000). There are a wide range of perspectives on what knowledge management entails, and this is not the place to rehearse them. Lougee's notion of federated collections represents a kind of knowledge management, as does the increasingly popular idea of institutional repositories. In general, knowledge management seems to consist of that set of activities that arise from the library's assumption of an expanded role in the chain of scholarly communication. These include the function of the library as creator, publisher, aggregator or distributor of scholarly material, as well as its role as an advocate and change agent for scholarly communication practices in general.

A couple of recent articles by Martin Dillon and Ross Atkinson talk about knowledge management and a potential way for libraries to use knowledge management to improve the productivity of users (Dillon, 2002; Atkinson, forthcoming). Dillon points out that universities do a very poor job of offering access to the intellectual capital of their organizations–the intellectual products produced by its faculty, students and research staff–and that libraries are in fact the responsible agency for rectifying this situation. Atkinson, in the context of discussing cooperative collection development, offers a similar observation. "Academic libraries know very little about the information being produced on their campuses . . . If libraries seriously intend to effect a system of knowledge management services, they . . . need to assemble dynamic information databases that summarize and track local research" and make these databases accessible to other institutions. He sees one value of such services as facilitation of collaboration by scholars in different institutions. Bibliographers, with their experience as subject experts and liaisons to academic programs, might play a natural, if not an essential, role in the development of the kind of knowledge management service described by Dillon and Atkinson.

This, of course, is but one, rather limited, manifestation of knowledge management. To look at another extreme, I am more uncertain about the role that subject librarians might play in the kind of information system described by Ian Foster in a talk summarized in a recent *RLG News* (Foster 2002). There he speaks about the potential of what he terms the grid distributed computing concept to transform scientific research. Like the grid that manages the distribution of electrical energy, an information grid would perform a similar function within a circumscribed field of study, like research on the human brain. Essential to achieving this potential are incredible increases in storage capacity and computer speed, combined with even greater increases in network performance. Foster uses the example of brain imaging to illustrate his point. He offers that not long ago you could image brains non-invasively at a centimeter resolution, resulting in three kilobytes of data. Now it is possible to image a brain at 10 microns, producing three terabytes of data for a scan. But the goal, he claims, is to track the location of individual cells, requiring one-micron resolution, and producing three petabytes of data for a single scan. When you have collected hundreds or thousands of scans for comparison, the concept of the grid becomes necessary, as a means of managing data, sharing computing capacity, and building knowledge. Foster is talking primarily about grids that function in disciplines like physics and astronomy, genomics, climatology, and the experimental sciences generally, but he suggests they could have great potential in the humanities and social sciences. The goals of the grid information systems he describes seem to be conceptually identical to the goals of a library–to provide access to information in order to enable the production of new information, or knowledge, by users. What is particularly interesting about this system is its inherently cooperative nature, and the fact that–as far as I know–the information it contains stands completely outside of the information systems managed by libraries. The emergence of information systems like the grids described by Foster clearly raises all sorts of issues with regard to preservation, and the sharing of information outside of the disciplinary, or even national, boundaries within which it was created.

As Foster's grid concept demonstrates, one challenge for the future lies in the breadth and mass of the universe of resources–the knowledge–to be managed. In spite, and in part because, of the dimensions of the challenge presented by these new models, there would seem to be a natural place for the skills of the collection management librarian in at least some areas of the knowledge management enterprise. The "ideal" bibliographer, we might say, has solid subject knowledge, an understanding of the literature of the field, and close connections with the faculty and students he or she serves. With the addition of good interpersonal skills, administrative support, and some technical knowledge (or access to someone else who has it), you may have an effective agent, as part of a team, for putting into practice the ideas of knowledge management. The selector would bring knowledge about the key players on campus, the local intellectual resources that might be appropriate targets for action, and the faculty who might be willing to cooperate in a federated venture, publishing program or repository project. But I wonder how many collection management practitioners are actively reinventing their jobs in this way.

If I am right that some collection development librarians are not eagerly embracing these new potential roles, it may be useful to ask "why." I suppose that one reason may be demographic. Recent statistics indicate that the average age of academic librarians is around fifty, this at a time when the profession needs staff of exceptional agility and flexibility. Longevity unfortunately brings not only the wisdom of experience, but also the inertia of longstanding habit. This is not to say that many in this age cohort have not eagerly embraced the possibilities of transforming libraries in response to the new environment. But it would be sanguine to assert that most were doing so. To make matters worse, there is growing concern that library schools, at current production rates of students entering academic librarianship, cannot possibly replace the people retiring in the next decade. Two areas of great stress, in fact, are area studies and science librarians, both specialties where subject knowledge is critical, if not essential.

Another factor discouraging the embrace of new roles results from the fact that libraries in general continue to ingest large amounts of print. While we hear much about the rapid growth of spending on electronic resources, most libraries still spend far more on traditionally published material. Aside from technical services staff, selectors are probably the group most engaged with this still important world of print. Dealing with it demands a considerable amount of their psychic and physical energy. Selectors (at least in many fields) are no less buried under the avalanche of publishers' brochures, flyers and approval slips–to which we can now add email solicitations–than they were ten or fifteen years ago.

If we attempt to stand somewhat outside this everyday world of the selector, where print remains deeply important, we might conclude, as Conway suggests, that "[t]oday's library is 'all digital' in the sense that all services and content (digital and non-digital) are mediated via web gateways" (Conway, 2002). Even more fundamental, it seems clear that sometime in the past few years, we have begun to see content on paper–books, journals and similar formats–refracted through the lens of digital information systems and digital delivery, rather than the other way around. That is, there has been an essential shift in perspective, such that we analogize the traditional print universe by way of the digital, instead of the opposite. But this shift, however profound, is not one that easily translates into a job description or organizational hierarchy.

When we think about the potential roles of selectors, there is also the problem of supply, of numbers. Before UCLA, my first job in a small college library involved little or no collection development. Faculty did most of the selection, supplemented by us librarians filling in gaps from *Choice* and a few other sources. Most academic libraries, including many of the smaller ARL members, have never had the luxury of selectors expert in all, or even most, of the areas they covered. I expect that subject specialists with advanced degrees or extensive subject background, outside of language-dependent area studies, are not very common outside of larger ARL libraries. If librarians, rather than faculty, do most selection, the typical selector covers far more subjects than any one person can know well. This is not to imply that non-specialists cannot do a highly competent job of collection development and management. But if we are considering the role of subject expertise in the realms of collection federation or knowledge management, there is a point at which the need for in-depth subject knowledge–beyond that required for day-to-day selection–becomes more important.

I recall hearing an informal talk at UCLA by a prominent, now retired library leader, where he tossed off the observation that he could imagine a research library of the future staffed by eighty to ninety subject specialists, together with a handful of technologists. Keep in mind that this was the mid-1980s, the era of mainframes and the introduction of the Macintosh, and well before most of us had heard of BITNET, much less the Internet. His notion appealed to me at the time, at least in part, because I was a subject specialist myself, and he was predicting that I might have a future. But this is clearly not the direction that most libraries are presently taking in terms of staffing. The proportions are likely in fact to be reversed, nor do we see many other specialties disappearing. As appealing as this vision might be to someone yearning for the golden age of bibliographers, it seems highly dubious as a future scenario.

While we sometimes worry about the short supply of technological expertise, I hear less often of concerns about the lack of subject specialists (outside of area studies and the sciences). Yet I suspect that the challenge of finding enough new people with subject knowledge who are interested in these embryonic library roles may be as acute a problem as the need for those presently on our staffs to develop new skills. The program recently announced by the Council on Library and Information Resources (CLIR) to "incorporate more academically trained professionals into the research library staff" seems to recognize this problem (Marcum 2003, 1 & 4). The program envisages a group of research libraries offering internships with a specified curriculum to young scholars at or near the end of doctoral studies, some in disciplinary specialties, others in functional specialties. At the end of the program each of the 10-12 individuals selected each year would be placed in academic libraries around the country with CLIR's help. This program sounds like a move in the right direction, but I can only wonder if it will be enough.

Of course, most of our institutions do have people on campus with the relevant subject knowledge in all the fields important to our institutions–namely, the faculty, along with their graduate student apprentices (at least in doctoral institutions). Perhaps we could tap the subject knowledge of faculty and graduate students in implementing knowledge management systems. In some instances, such as the grid systems described by Foster, they are already moving in this direction with little or no help from us. The challenge will be to capture enough of their deeply fragmented attention, and get them interested in this enterprise, so that resources–in particular their time or that of their graduate students–are directed to these ends.

CONCLUSION

I have looked at some future paths for collection management in the digital age, and tried to envision how the skills of collection development librarians–by whatever name–might contribute to those futures. The subject expertise characteristic of selectors can play an important role as libraries seek to develop functional portals, implement federated collections, manage the chaos of the Web, and meet the challenges of the knowledge management enterprise. For this subject knowledge to be applied successfully, libraries and their subject specialists must overcome formidable obstacles and barriers, including the realities of demographics, the distracting presence of large amounts of print, and a limited supply of the kind of deep subject knowledge that will be required. It is too early to say if nascent responses to the supply problem will be effective, while attempts to draw on the time and expertise of faculty promise mixed success.

Another solution for the scarcity of qualified subject specialists lies in cooperation. In a thought-provoking paper given at the CRL-sponsored Aberdeen Woods conference (to be published in the next volume of *Collection Management*), Ross Atkinson revisits what he terms the "seemingly interminable discussion of cooperative collection development." In the end he concludes that cooperation can serve the goals of library knowledge management in a variety of ways. This is not the place to summarize his arguments about all of the ways that libraries might cooperate to provide knowledge management services. What is germane to the discussion here is that the best opportunity to tap the subject expertise necessary to realize knowledge management–and many of the other new roles for collection management and development I have mentioned–may come by sharing the time and energy of the subject experts scattered among our libraries, and those we are able to attract in the future. Given the spotty track record of cooperation when books and journals, rather than people, were the objects of cooperation, it is easy to be cynical about the chances of success. Nevertheless, such an approach seems to offer the best chance of making real progress.

REFERENCES

ARL. 2002. "Collections & Access for the 21st Century Scholar: Changing Roles of Research Libraries," *ARL: A Bimonthly Report on Research Library Issues and Actions from ARL, CNI and SPARC*, no. 225 (December).

Atkinson, Ross (forthcoming). "Uses and Abuses of Cooperation in a Digital Age." *Collection Management* 28 (1-2).

Branin, Joseph, Groen, Frances and Thorin, Suzanne 2000. "The Changing Nature of Collection Management in Research Libraries," *Library Resources and Technical Services* 44 (1), 23-32.

Conway, Paul 2002. "Towards a Shared Vision of Content Management in the Web Environment: An Outline of Concepts and Definitions" [Online]. Available: http://www.arl.org/collectaccess/CAconway.html [2003, February 23].

Dillon, Martin 2002. "Knowledge Management: Chimera or Solution?" *portal: Libraries and the Academy* 2, 321-336.

Foster, Ian 2002. "The Grid: Enabling Resource Sharing within Virtual Organizations," *Research Libraries Group News* 55 (Fall), 9-13.

Hazen, Dan 2000. "Twilight of the Gods? Bibliographers in the Electronic Age," *Library Trends* 48 (Spring), 821-841.

Lougee, Wendy Pradt. 2002. *Diffuse Libraries: Emergent Roles for the Research Library in the Digital Age*, Washington, D.C.: Council on Library and Information Resources.

Marcum, Deanna B. 2003. "CLIR's Direction for 2003," *CLIR Issues*, 31 (January/February), 1 & 4.

Are We All Global Librarians Now?

Alice Prochaska

INTRODUCTION

In the digital environment, the potent opportunities of partnerships both national and international place the great international research libraries within several overlapping communities. Our institutional boundaries have exploded, and our assumptions are challenged. The concept of national and international library collections demands to be re-examined at a time when the Internet is facilitating not only local access to global collections but its corollary, global access to local collections.

This paper will focus on some international dimensions of digital access to library materials, but it is rooted in and mainly derived from my own experience in two different national arenas: those of the United Kingdom and the United States.

In the various forums I frequent, a consensus seems to me to be developing, that focuses on content at least as much as on the vehicles and standards for giving access to content. This is not to say that the library and information communities have cracked the thorny issues of providing reliable access to digitized materials: on the contrary, new opportunities in the open archiving environment raise at least as many questions as they solve. (Top of the list for many, perhaps most of us, is the problem of long-term digital preservation.) But a

---

Alice Prochaska is University Librarian, Yale University Library, New Haven, CT (E-mail: alice.prochaska@yale.edu).

[Haworth co-indexing entry note]: "Are We All Global Librarians Now?" Prochaska, Alice. Co-published simultaneously in *Journal of Library Administration* (The Haworth Information Press, an imprint of The Haworth Press, Inc.) Vol. 39, No. 4, 2003, pp. 79-88; and: *Improved Access to Information: Portals, Content Selection, and Digital Information* (ed: Sul H. Lee) The Haworth Information Press, an imprint of The Haworth Press, Inc., 2003, pp. 79-88. Single or multiple copies of this article are available for a fee from The Haworth Document Delivery Service [1-800-HAWORTH, 9:00 a.m. - 5:00 p.m. (EST). E-mail address: docdelivery@haworthpress.com].

http://www.haworthpress.com/web/JLA
© 2003 by The Haworth Press, Inc. All rights reserved.
Digital Object Identifier: 10.1300/J111v39n04_08

myriad of opportunities is calling forth a galaxy of responses. The riches of digitized resources pile up, challenging our budgets and our cataloging capabilities, and at the same time vastly expanding the appetite of library users for more and more ready access to more and more enticing material. The new forms of library support that we are providing, and the increasingly high quality of that support, lead our readers in endlessly extensible explorations toward new questions, new answers and new ways of combining information to create new knowledge.

THE COMMUNITIES WE SERVE

One way to begin on a reflection about the role of digitized library content is to think about the changing character of the communities we serve. Libraries do serve communities, and increasingly they are virtual communities of unseen users, downloading material from the Internet at will, for use in ways that we, the content providers, cannot foresee or know. A subsidiary question is: whether we should really be talking about "communities" at all, or should we imagine individuals working in cell-like isolation? Students increasingly can work alone in their rooms if they want to, borrowing fewer books, asking fewer questions face-to-face at reference desks, defining their reference needs by what they can find on their computer screens. Library statistics suggest that these trends are not necessarily developing as we might have predicted. Still, the more content we provide in digitized form, the more likely we are to become instrumental in changing the former communities of learning and reading that are familiar to us. We need to understand that transformation and our many possible roles in shaping it.

The question of communities begs many questions about the definition of a community of library users in the twenty-first century. It brings us back to the physical community, the town, the university, the learned society, the nation, that supports any particular library. And it expands the horizon toward a vision of the greater community of potential readers that libraries can now reach.

I propose to devote most of this talk to the expanding horizon, but before launching on that trajectory, a few words are in order about our existing communities. I am reminded every day, in my work as Yale University Librarian, that the university regards its library as its own. A vital part of my job is to foster and develop the relationship between the library, represented by its staff and its collections, and the faculty, students and staff at Yale. I contemplate the intractable problems of overflowing stacks and catalog backlogs, complex issues to do with the management and preservation of a vast circulating collection, and a collection development budget on which exploding electronic opportunities and the still-growing output of publications in traditional format place huge demands. I look at the enormous challenges of renovating the library's physical spaces to keep them up to modern standards. These problems are common to just about every research library in the nation, and unless we overcome them, whatever we achieve in the digital arena will be seen by our home communities as of secondary importance at best. Our recently formulated strategic plan at Yale states the blindingly obvious: "Access to collections is our driving force." If the definition of collections in that formulation is protean, including everything from licensed scientific databases to ancient papyri, "access" means first and foremost access, in every medium, for the Yale community. Similar remarks, allowing for different descriptions of their local and institutional setting, apply to just about any type of library you care to name.

James Billington, giving the Ditchley Foundation lecture to an invited audience in England in the summer of 2000, addressed the question of communities in a way that should give pause to all western librarians, and especially those from English-speaking cultures.[1] He lamented the cultural imperialism of the Internet, and sharply criticized what he called the "troubadours of the new culture" for rejoicing "in the prospect of a streamlined basic English becoming not just a lingua-franca but a vehicle for genuine human brotherhood." What these "troubadours" fail to realize according to Dr. Billington, is that if the "Pidgin-English monolinguism of the air traffic controller and the computer programmer" is permitted to dominate the Internet, it will cut us off "not just from the billions who speak other languages, but also from any real understanding of the English literary and historical heritage." He went on to refer to Gene Rochlin's vision, in his influential book *Trapped in the Net*, of the Internet spreading authority everywhere, but locating responsibility nowhere. I do not agree that the Internet is turning out to be monolingual at all, but Dr. Billington's admonition is well taken.

He was referring to access to publications both current and from the past, and in the widest possible sense. If we turn our attention to one small but burgeoning sector of the digital universe, the digitization of unique historic originals, some difficult issues about community in the digital library world come sharply into focus.

For instance, it is now possible to provide high-quality surrogates for the world's great treasures of art and text. This capability changes the nature of the debate about "cultural restitution" or repatriation of unique manuscript items from other cultures that are held in our collections. Some examples from my own experience illustrate a phenomenon that is increasingly familiar to museums and libraries all over the world. Innumerable items held within the British Library's special collections are potentially subject to claims from other parts of the world. The subjects of current claims include sacred Ethiopian manuscripts seized from the emperor Tewodoros at the Battle of Magdala in 1868, the Codex Sinaiticus, virtually the earliest written version of the gospels, which is claimed by St. Catherine's Monastery in Sinai, a 12th-century missal from Benevento in Italy, which migrated from there to Britain in mysterious circumstances after the Second World War, and the Lindisfarne Gospels, the greatest surviving example of Anglo-Saxon graphic art.

The case of the Lindisfarne Gospels contains within it many of the questions about communities and ownership that perplex politicians and the custodians of unique historic materials alike. This intricately illuminated volume, a work of art from the turn of the eighth to ninth centuries AD, is the subject of an energetic campaign not in another country, but by people representing the northeast of England. Fueled by the strong trend toward regionalism in current British politics, local politicians and media have led at least one expedition to London to hold a vigil in the British Library's exhibition galleries on March 20, the feast of St. Cuthbert in whose honor the manuscript was created some 1,200 years ago, almost certainly by monks on the Island of Lindisfarne. The northeast English regional press is adamant that ownership of this treasure belongs in the northeast, and that is where it should reside. Three different sites contest exactly where the treasure should be kept; but they are unanimous that it is wrong for the "arrogant metropolitan" people at the British Library to hang on to it.

The British Library's position is that this sacred treasure also has iconic significance for the thousands of international visitors who come to London every year to see the many original works of early Christian art and text displayed together in the Library's gallery. As a resource for scholars, it is housed with kindred materials from other regions, which scholars benefit from seeing together, not to mention its proximity to all of the published material they need to use in conjunction with it. Moreover, the curatorial and technical resources of the Library itself are brought to bear, giving the manuscript the best possible care, in conditions that are hugely expensive to create, and only economic for organizations where a critical mass of materials can be housed in one place. Recently, the curator of medieval manuscripts, Dr. Michelle Brown, carried out research using high resolution digital imaging to reveal the artist's marks of drafting on the reverse of the vellum pages, and traced evidence that led her to ascribe the manuscript to a slightly later date, bringing it within the active lifetime of the great Anglo-Saxon scholar Bede. Raman spectroscopy, another electronic technique which makes it possible to test the pigment of works of art without having to remove microscopic samples, has demonstrated that some of the blue pigment used by the Lindisfarne artist was lapis lazuli, which is thought to have been available at that time only in the area of modern Afghanistan. Taken together with the clear Byzantine influences on the art work, this raises important questions about the transfer of goods and techniques across the world in the early medieval period.

While robustly justifying its retention of this manuscript, the British Library also uses digitization in an effort to meet the demand for widespread access, and the Lindisfarne Gospels was the first item to be mounted on its pioneering "Turning the Pages" technology, with CD-ROM access following. Digitization itself is a double-edged weapon in the argument, however, as it leads the campaigners to propose that the British Library and its visitors no longer need to keep the original.

All great research libraries deploy huge resources to preserve their holdings both for research and for the wider public. There are good scholarly arguments for holding a critical mass of material in one place where unique items can be compared and studied together. And yet, we must remain sensitive to the fact that even the most wonderful electronic version is not the original. The manuscript itself, like so many other survivals from the past, has its own unique value. It contains information that cannot be reproduced; and it is iconic, symbolic, irreplaceable. As far as the arguments about cultural restitution go, we have to take our stand on the nature and role of international collections, the cost-effective application of rare expertise and expensive provision for preservation, and the value an international audience places on seeing these treasures together. Even digitization cannot perform the magic of locating the original in two places at once. So the issue of whose community the manuscript belongs to remains a matter of dispute. Our job, it seems to me, is to create the widest possible community of people who appreciate and benefit from these treasures. The library of the 21st century faces the challenge to do this job better than libraries have ever done before.

CREATING COMMUNITIES

Building a community of users, and connecting with that community, is among the most rewarding work open to a librarian. Archivists, bibliographers, catalogers, reference librarians and subject specialists are all in different ways involved in this work, and so too are the IT specialists and systems librarians. I suspect we all share the professional ideal of supporting and developing the librarian's role as an active curator or mediator. In the model I have in mind, the librarian or curator seeks out new opportunities to bring library collections to a wider audience, and enters into dialog with an intelligent public about the ways the material might be used. Thanks to the Internet we are able, at a cost, to share collections internationally and not only among scholars and seasoned aficionados, but also with members of the wider public, "lifelong learners," schools, family historians, and many others. Most libraries that hold rare collections are building new skill-sets in order to present parts of their collections in electronic form, suitably selected, interpreted and in context.

The British Library again provides a useful example of this form of outreach. Its *In Place* web site[2] describes a project funded by National Lottery money, which will digitize parts of the British Library collection for free use by the public as part of a broader UK project costing a total of more than $75 million. Two from a total of eighteen collection descriptions give a flavor of the principles underlying the British Library part of this project. Of its selection of illuminated medieval manuscripts, it says: "Too fragile to be made physically available to many, *In Place* makes these treasures electronically accessible to the communities that once produced or owned them." Another collection, entitled *Svidesh Vadesh* (a phrase meaning "Home away from Home") draws on the holdings of the former India Office Library and Records: "This remarkable resource presents the cultural heritage of one of the country's largest ethnic groups and also meets the needs of a wider academic community in Britain and beyond." The purpose behind the *In Place* project is one shared by hundreds, perhaps thousands, of libraries world-wide.

Meanwhile, to give just one instance of a mature and much admired project closer to home (one in which I can claim no part), the University of North Carolina's *Documenting the American South* web site provides a superb example of what can be achieved through the marriage of academic and popular objectives. To quote from the introductory page, this site "provides access to digitized primary materials that offer Southern perspectives on American history and culture. It supplies teachers, students, and researchers at every educational level with a wide array of titles they can use for reference, studying, teaching, and research. Currently, *DAS* includes six digitization projects: slave narratives, first-person narratives, Southern literature, Confederate imprints, materials related to the church in the black community, and North Caroliniana."

An aspect of *Documenting the American South* that impresses me particularly is the inclusion of a feedback mechanism, and examples of comments from users.[3] Some of you may have visited it, and I know it is used on the Yale campus among others for teaching history of the American South. A compilation of some of the feedback, mounted on the web site, contains moving testimony to the importance of this material for members of the general public, schools, and others in addition to academic users. There is a whole section of comments from overseas, including this from a student in Poland writing an MA thesis on Alice Walker: "Thanks to your collection I finally was able to go through several texts which gave me sort of overall view . . . And I am really grateful because my university library lacks American sources, and generally it's really hard to find anything concerning Black Americans . . ."

An international research library gains immeasurably from dialog not only with its most regular users but with visitors from further afield. Expertise has become international; and now all the more so in the digital era. Not only that, but the parent universities of many of the leading research libraries are pursuing an increasingly aggressive international agenda. Yale has announced its intention to make its fourth century the one in which the university becomes truly international. The Yale Center for International and Area Studies and its offspring, the Center for the Study of Globalization (headed by a former President of Mexico, Ernesto Zedillo), are only two high-profile manifestations of this international agenda. Last week the university launched its new web site, Yale and the World,[4] accompanied by a substantial paper handout on Reference Materials.

The introduction to the library's section of this publication illustrates how we have tried to position ourselves within Yale's international community:

> The Yale University Library, rated among the ten largest libraries in the world, has been international in its scope since the university was founded. Today, more than 50% of additions to the general collections come from outside the United States, and the Library's area studies and special collections are notably rich in primary sources for the study of foreign languages, cultures and civilizations. Electronic databases add enormously to the international material available for the Yale community to use.

> All parts of the University Library system support international study actively: librarians travel overseas to collect material, and work closely with the relevant faculty departments to provide bibliographic and instructional support, and to ensure that the collections are as wide-ranging and current as possible. A growing number of fellowships bring world scholars to Yale specifically to use Library collections. Librarian interns also come from different parts of the world; and Yale librarians in turn participate in international organizations such as the International Federation of Library Associations, numerous subject-based library organizations, and as members of world-wide academic communities. Some specific partnerships (e.g., one established in 2002 with the World Health Organization's HINARI scheme to support access to networked public health information in developing countries) spread the benefits of the university's expertise. The library maintains close links with international publishers and other information providers.

> Much of the work of individual Yale librarians, in these and other forums, is directed towards international activities such as monitoring access to government documents, participating in the education of research

librarians, establishing international standards for the preservation and care of rare books and manuscripts, contributing to exhibitions and publications overseas, sharing in programs of digitization, and taking part in conferences that promote free access to information.

The library's contribution to the university's international agenda thus suffuses the work of the university; and it needs to be seen to do that. In turn, the presence of representatives of an international research community is a vital resource for the librarian to use, to test and develop the services that reach out to people beyond the physical precincts of the library itself. It is one way, but perhaps not the most critical. The library of the future will reach out to its local community, to its state, regional and national communities, in new ways, as well as expanding its horizons around the globe. Libraries have now, and the great research libraries above all others, the chance and the challenge to build up collections for world-wide audiences *and* at the same time, to bring world-wide collections and international usages into the local community in which they are rooted. Above all, library communities are created by mutual comprehension, and by a whole range of working partnerships founded on that comprehension. And that comes from librarians and the users of libraries coming together, in both physical and virtual space, to discuss their use of the collections, and so to understand better the potential of those irreplaceable assets, the collections themselves.

PRACTICALITIES

To aspire to international access in the digital environment is good. To be conscious of our professional and ethical reasons for doing so is vital. How, in reality, do we achieve the connections and community building that we can all agree are so desirable? I will not venture on to territory where other speakers are so much more expert than I, but a few general observations about good practice may be in order.

First, it is crucially important not only to adhere to technical and descriptive standards, but also to make those standards explicit. Both the *Documenting the American South* and *In Place* projects do that. The *DAS* web site includes a digitizing narrative arranged under the following headings: Standards, Methodology, Remote Access, Scanning Images, Copyright, Preservation, Archiving, OCR scanning, and Encoding guidelines. Rigorous attention to all of those aspects of any large-scale digitizing project is fundamental, not only to achieving the initial usable collection of digitized materials, but also to creating a collection that will endure and that can be used by multiple individuals and constituencies, for multiple purposes. If there is one basic reason for undertaking such projects, it surely must be their capacity to enhance access for a plurality of users.

Second, a common feature of most good web sites now is the provision of a mechanism for feedback. If we are seriously aiming to provide an environment of learning and discovery in which new communities will arise, we can only succeed by learning about those communities and learning from them. Given the extraordinary costs and often the still speculative nature of the projects we are undertaking, it seems to me that measures of customer satisfaction are mandatory. Creating such measures is no easy matter, especially when you consider that all of us are building these great projects for universal access on the basis of local cultural norms. International standards like Dublin Core and its successors provide a common platform of accessibility, but the content itself will remain gloriously and intractably, itself. The explanation of vocabulary in an international environment, the use of historic language, or of imperfectly understood foreign languages, description of images that could be interpreted in many different ways: these are just some of the problems that challenge us as intermediaries between the contents of our digitized collections, and a remote and unseen audience.

A third challenge in the web universe, is that of navigation. Here again, others have spent careers grappling with this challenge. All I wish to say here is that the newest generation of linking and harvesting technologies do give us an opportunity to navigate intelligently amongst the galaxies of available material. These are vital tools for content providers and content users alike. We need to pay close attention to all of the other material that is out there, overlapping with what we plan to provide, answering the questions we thought we wanted to answer, offering materials for the same users we wish to address. As citizens of this particular community of content providers, we should also be conscious of our obligation to post information about what we do in places where others can find it. Registries of digital standards, and registries of digital projects and existing collections, are surprisingly difficult to create, and we could all do with a manual on how to create and share this sort of information. Reinventing the wheel is a common enough problem, but reinventing the space shuttle is infinitely more costly.

That leads to the fourth and last aspect of practical support for far-reaching digitization programs that I would like to mention here: partnerships. Everyone present at this conference must be involved in several partnerships of one sort or another: sharing between different organizations on campus, sharing between universities, between university libraries and other research libraries, between museums, archives and libraries, and sharing across international divisions, sometimes across linguistic ones.

Partnerships between organizations can be difficult to set up and hard to sustain. Often motivated by institutional agendas that prove not to be compatible, sometimes forced by the requirements of foundations and other grant-giving bodies, rather than springing from the organic relationships between collections, curators or librarians and users that still form the paradigm most of us grew up with: these are some of the forms of partnership most of us will have struggled to set up at one time or another, and often we will have fallen short of our objectives, or failed outright. It is no coincidence that the two projects I have used as leading examples of successful digitization for a mass audience, are both founded firmly within a single library. In the case of the British Library's *In Place* project, the prehistory includes a partnership of multiple organizations, most of which fell by the wayside or are now only loosely federated, if at all, with the lead one.

Nevertheless, for all sorts of good reasons, partnerships remain a desirable model in this environment. It is here that organizations like the Digital Library Federation, OCLC, the Research Libraries Group, and perhaps above all the looser grouping of the Association of Research Libraries, can and do make a huge difference. Like other speakers here, I am involved with the Global Resources program of the ARL, and with the strategic planning effort that is currently under way at the DLF. My library is also one of those that are committed to contribute digital content to RLG's Cultural Materials Alliance, but has not yet done so. All of these programs confront their own problems, some different and some common to all three. It would take another paper, perhaps another conference, to analyze the obstacles to progress that all of us could describe. But the point I wish to make here, and this is where I want to end, is that collectively we, the custodians of the world's memory, have found it necessary to group together and pool our resources. We do need to draw on each other's experience as well as each other's collections, and the underlying objective of enhancing access to those collections motivates us to keep working on the partnerships. Whatever the practical barriers to high quality access, there is, I believe, a consensus that we can solve those problems together, and that I suppose, is why we are all here.

NOTES

    1. James H. Billington, "The Human Consequences of the Information Revolution," Ditchley Foundation lecture XXXVII, in Supplement to the *Ditchley Conference Reports 2000/01*, Chipping Norton, UK: The Ditchley Foundaiton, 2001.
    2. http://www.bl.uk/about/inplaceintro.html.
    3. http://docsouth.unc.edu/aboutdas.html.
    4. http://world.yale.edu/.

Portals and the Human Factor: Bringing Virtual Services to the Life of the Mind or the Scholarly Stargate

Barbara I. Dewey

INTRODUCTION TO THE SCHOLARLY STARGATE

An entry point, a door, an opening, an entrance. The concept of portal must contain action. In order for it to be relevant someone or something has to go through it to the other side. This action and interaction with the portal reminds me of the movie *Stargate*. The portal is like the perimeter of the stargate and traveling through its center is like navigating to needed resources and services. The act of entering the center is difficult yet flexible. The other side can be straightforward or complex. An earthlike and understandable world or a world that is totally incomprehensible to the traveler may be the destination.

Until recently the notion of a scholarly portal focused mainly on content and methods of accessing that content. This paper will explore the portal in terms of services meant to aid the user or traveler not only to go through successfully but also locate and apply its content to scholarship and learning, or the life of the mind. After a review of the literature, single and multiple portals will be examined since the stargate in question is often multiple in nature. Maybe there are two or three stargates or maybe the center part has several layers. Services addressing integration within and between portals will be discussed. Examples

Barbara I. Dewey is Dean of Libraries, University of Tennessee, Knoxville, TN (E-mail: bdewey@utk.edu).

[Haworth co-indexing entry note]: "Portals and the Human Factor: Bringing Virtual Services to the Life of the Mind or the Scholarly Stargate." Dewey, Barbara I. Co-published simultaneously in *Journal of Library Administration* (The Haworth Information Press, an imprint of The Haworth Press, Inc.) Vol. 39, No. 4, 2003, pp. 89-101; and: *Improved Access to Information: Portals, Content Selection, and Digital Information* (ed: Sul H. Lee) The Haworth Information Press, an imprint of The Haworth Press, Inc., 2003, pp. 89-101. Single or multiple copies of this article are available for a fee from The Haworth Document Delivery Service [1-800-HAWORTH, 9:00 a.m. - 5:00 p.m. (EST). E-mail address: docdelivery@haworthpress.com].

http://www.haworthpress.com/web/JLA
© 2003 by The Haworth Press, Inc. All rights reserved.
Digital Object Identifier: 10.1300/J111v39n04_09

of institutional and multi-institutional portal building from the research library community and how they relate to digital library initiatives will provide a way for us to look at how action or user interaction is addressed. Next steps, opportunities, and challenges for both sharpening and expanding the scholarly portal or stargate will conclude the paper.

THE SCHOLARS PORTAL CONCEPT

The concept of a scholars portal is well-described by Jerry Campbell in a thought piece to jumpstart what would become the ARL Scholars Portal Project and launch many other discussions and initiatives regarding a portal for the scholarly teaching and learning community. Campbell describes a new integrated digital library through the scholars portal concept:

> The *scholars portal* would facilitate the addition of high-quality material by fostering standards, searching across databases, and offering a variety of supporting tools. As a result, libraries, corporations, and many other organizations would be empowered to contribute to an accessible, distributed digital library. The existence and efforts of *scholars portal*, therefore, would accelerate the growth of high-quality material and facilitate what has been referred to as the global relational research library.[1]

Campbell's concept of a portal leading to a digital library that transcends a local online catalog with a smattering of reformatted digital collections is taking hold. The scholars portal concept puts a frame on the new integrated digital library and provides a context for concrete development of such capabilities. Perhaps it's like our stargate perimeter with integrated services.

Sarah Thomas, University Librarian at Cornell, has developed another view of the portal concept. She describes the ideal discovery tool as "one which consults omnivorously, but which returns a selection of relevant results in rapid sequence. Searchers find out what they need promptly without having to wade through a vast assortment of tangentially related, inaccurate, or otherwise deficient data."[2] Thomas' concept, largely a combination of powerful portal and highly accurate search engine, is the basis of a robust digital library.

Mary Jackson will talk more about the ARL project and the surveys she's done on portal functionality, but clearly there are at least two themes for current portal development in terms of virtual service tools to support content–the development and implementation of multiple source search engine tools and the existence of at least one supporting service for the user if not many.[3]

PORTAL DEVELOPMENT LITERATURE

The research and professional literature on portals is rapidly emerging from a variety of perspectives–e-business applications, library interpretations, and campus views. A challenge in reviewing the literature is the diversity of content under the umbrella title "portal." For the purposes of this paper service elements in current writings about portals are examined to provide a framework for discussing the scholarly stargate's contribution to the life of the mind. An interesting sidebar is that after this paper was begun the University of Tennessee decided, as part of an undergraduate enrichment process, to have every freshman read a book and this program is called "Life of the Mind." In 2003, the inaugural year, the chosen book is James McBride's *The Color of Water*.[4] In this case the book is seen as the portal into the university experience.

E-BUSINESS PERSPECTIVE

From an e-business perspective portals are often seen as frameworks or architecture on which information sits, and where integration of data and applications can take place. Saha's definition of portal from the e-business perspective is: "a portal is a single integrated point of comprehensive, ubiquitous, and useful access to information (data) applications, and people."[5] He describes portals as providing a full range of services. He notes portal types including *corporate* with business intelligence, knowledge management, and customer-relationship management capabilities; *inter-enterprise* which can deal with chains of business or are more consortial in nature providing information from a large number of sources such as suppliers, and services to help manage/coordinate the business processes needed to keep the chain together; *e-marketplaces* span enterprises supporting a industry-wide perspective and can support such services as bidding; *personal* portals and *community* portals provide a customized first point of access, and *ASP* (*Application, Service Providers*) provide integrated access to data and applications supplemented by a set of additional services. Services outlined in the Saha paper are under six categories: content management, applications collaboration, access and integration, presentation, and system management.

LIBRARY/EDUCATION PERSPECTIVE

Literature on portals and portal services in libraries and education, while linking to the e-business portal literature, relates more to content and audience. Library portal literature can be found under such headings as "digital libraries," "institutional repositories," and "learning technologies." A few examples are noted here. One major category of literature focuses on subject portals where European efforts are distinctive. Clark talks about the vision of an initiative funded by the Joint Information Systems Committee or JISC called the Resource Discovery Network (RDN). RDN's goal is to empower higher education by "providing quick, coherent and reliable access to a managed information environment geared to support learning and teaching activities."[6] A major focus is the development of subject portals. In terms of service, the Hubs, as they are called, offer:

- customizable home pages driven by a single secure log in
- ability to share information and communicate across the community that is using the hub
- transparent access to wide range of high-quality information deemed to be of relevance
- ease of use and ubiquitous availability
- access to information located in disparate locations

The emphasis is on searchable content with a theme and cross-community searching, but no other services are mentioned in this context.

Heery, Carpenter, and Day summarize another level of this effort, a portal of multiple subject portals. The Renardus Project means to "establish a collaborative framework for European subject gateways" by gaining access to those that exist and figure out standardized access.[7] The primary service aspect seems to be subject aggregation and federating searching. Another approach is illustrated by the Subject Portals of the U.S. Department of Energy, Office of Scientific and Technical Information (OSTI).[8] This approach features distributed searching across a select set of heterogeneous databases plus a customized look and feel related to the sponsoring organization, still primarily focused on service of discipline-based content.

An alternative take on the specialized portal is to target not only specific subject areas but also develop functionality for a specific population. This approach may have benefits for the higher education community as well. Large, Beheshti, and Cole present a matrix intended to serve as a tool for designing the architecture of a web portal logically and systematically. Their specific application was a children's web portal in a museum.[9] The architecture in this example includes three major areas–the interface, interactiveness, and retrieval with the goal of linking this portal's purpose and design objectives to its actual design. The framework described in this study is intended as a model for optimization for targeted group effectiveness, in this case for a younger population. The notion of structuring a portal around user needs is fundamental when focusing on services.

Optimization leads to another area of library portal development, the customized view or personalization tools. Ghaphery reviews a three-year evaluation of Virginia Commonwealth University's MyLibrary, a personalization tool that permits library users to consolidate frequently used library resources and services.[10] A unified package of services is the goal for this and other MyLibrary-type applications. Integration into online course websites is another approach described by VCU. As Ghaphery notes, "The real mark of success in this vein would be a transparency of the MyLibrary service whereby patrons have unfettered access to customized library resources and services depending on their information needed. In the context of a class led by a professor or librarian, selected resources would sit freely and prominently alongside online course syllabi. For more general library use, a secure and single login would offer individual users a robust portal to digital content and service."

One aspect of the customized MyLibrary concept as it is commonly implemented is that some users may not want to be limited by, for example, database choices and prefer to continue using the general library website. Portal service development should keep this in mind as well as the concern that users will not keep up their profile. It remains unclear whether automatic SDI-type services will satisfy this concern, and whether these services could reach content beyond local library holdings into other scholarly venues.

INSTITUTIONAL PORTALS

The concept of institutional portal discussed by Dolphin, Miller, and Sherratt is defined as "a layer, which aggregates, integrates, personalizes and presents information, transactions and applications to the user according to their role and preferences."[11] This article notes that in order to effectively meet the needs of users portals should go beyond content and have the capability of integrating and aggregating a range of services and related functions. These services include:

- transparent logins
- mapping access rights presenting seamless access to user
- personalization of the content for display and the manner of display
- personalization within applications available on a portal
- integration with virtual learning environments

These concepts do relate more closely to the scholarly portal vision with increased emphasis of service and ease from the user's perspective. The institutional portal literature also focuses on the portal in a teaching and learning context.

TEACHING AND LEARNING

Application of portals to teaching and learning provides a framework for the extension of the classroom or a virtual classroom. The integration of scholarly (library) content, whether connected to the library or somewhere else, is becoming more common. Integration of services related to the content is beginning in learning management systems such as Blackboard and WebCT. Another aspect of the teaching and learning application includes recognition by general subject portal developers to include teaching and learning applications. For example, EEVL, a portal Hub of the Resource Discovery Network (described earlier), for engineering, mathematics and computing, features a new service called SearchLT Engineering. Its purpose is to help faculty select and access appropriate computer and web-based learning materials in engineering for courses. The service includes an evaluation component. Other services include a My Account feature allowing personalization, email alerts, saved searches, and other information.[12] In effect it is a science teacher's online curriculum library.

Integrated information literacy programs can also be part of a portal where instruction and guidance is an integral part of content. Although most libraries have web-based tutorials and other user education type programs on their website more integration is needed between the instructional programs, databases or resources in question, and virtual services where direct interaction with library personnel occurs. Imagine a portal where the acquisition of information literacy skills is imbedded or at least adjacent to discovery tools. Imagine the system has automatic testing and feedback capabilities and that all of this can be integrated into course websites.

DIGITAL LIBRARY DEVELOPMENT AND PORTALS

The concept of the digital library is deeply related to portal development and the new digital library architecture encompasses not only a wide variety of content but services and communication features as well. More than content, the emerging digital library also contains an interactive and collaborative component. Tochtermann talks about building the communication aspect of digital libraries to mirror the collaborative and highly interactive use of traditional libraries.[13] The digital library as a device for communication including accompanying services between faculty, students, and others is now a reality through chat rooms, electronic mail, interactive learning environments and the like.

The new digital library goes beyond traditional library boundaries and embraces collegiate or department-based digital resources and services of importance to students and faculty. Identifying rich campus-wide resources currently sitting in isolation of potential local and remote users is a great challenge. These resources include everything from image collections, digitized map data, specialized indexes, art portfolios to technical report literature. Creators often want these materials to be widely available but need a more integrated campus initiative to make that happen. Certainly a portal overlay, if you will, is necessary to provide the stargate structure to go through to these various resources in an efficient and effective way. And, as an overlay we are now creating ways to create as well as ways to react to and interact with existing resources.

Lougee talks about the emergence of the library as a diffuse agent. She describes an evolutionary process where libraries have adopted distributed models for information access and management, and more collaborative, open models for developing content and services. She asserts that "rather than being defined by its collections or the services that support them, the library can become a diffuse agent within the scholarly community."[14] Deep engagement using distributed technologies is possible in the creation and dissemination of knowledge. This goes beyond the reactive model of providing content and services for existing knowledge.

Is a scholarly portal the same thing as a digital library? Is a scholarly portal the same thing as an online catalog? Does it matter? I believe we are using these terms interactively because both portal and library include architecture for services and content. For example, at the University of Tennessee our digital library initiative concept encompasses services, content, and content beyond the "library." We've developed a chart to visually show the vision of the digital library, and it demonstrates the gateway aspect of the concept. It also provides a way to show how services are integrated into the process. The chart is out of date and overly limiting even before it is completed because it does not include all of the campus resources and services that should be connected to the digital library. It does not include all of the connections to collections and collaborative services linking Tennessee to other institutions. It does not include all of the portal-type features of various catalogs and databases such as linking, information management tools, etc. A second chart was developed which extends the scope to campus-wide and community scholarly resources such as Oak Ridge National Laboratory but it is still too limiting. Perhaps the ultimate service goal for our scholarly portal should be a continuous attempt to provide extensions to the scholarly community at large with the capability, not only of providing service to, but keeping track of these extensions by discipline or topic.

PORTAL AS PUBLISHER

A major aspect of diffuse agent model is library as publisher and at an even broader level library as institutional repository. Accompanying these roles are services to support and extend creation and dissemination of the content. Thus, the life of the mind is not only reflective but also interactive and creative. The new digital library architecture is also dynamic and interactive. Creation of new knowledge directly by the author to the reader and/or by an electronic scholarly publishing process constitutes a new dimension for library service and usage. Librarians and technologists can work together to develop ways for the creator of content to make it available to the campus and beyond. An example is the University of Iowa's Bailiwick, a web space for research-based web publications where authors retain full editorial control of their content and "where academic passions can be realized."[15] California Polytechnic features a system called Caltech CODA (Collection of Open Digital Archives) which now includes a number of different repositories of locally produced scholarship using electronic archiving software[16] where faculty can deposit research reports or other scholarly works in electronic format with appropriate metadata so the material can be accessed. The University of Michigan is producing a large number of "born digital" journals and digitized text collections. The University of Tennessee's Scholars Archive has begun with a partnership to publish backfiles of an existing journal.

The ability to create and deposit scholarly output and engage in electronic publishing offers a new, transformational role for colleges and universities in the scholarly communication process. Institutional repositories are the internal component of this interactive ability to publish and share. Ohio State's Knowledge Bank provides a vision of combining a scholarly portal with an institutional repository. "In the broadest sense, the Knowledge Bank can be said to include the full array of digital assets and information services available to or being created by OSU faculty, staff, and students." The "Knowledge Bank" is envisioned as both a "referatory" providing links to digital objects and a repository capable of archiving the increasing volume of digital content created at OSU for long-term use, dissemination, and preservation. Projects of this ambition will, no doubt, include many services to navigate through and manage these resources.[17]

INTERACTIVE SPACES

The scholarly portal can include dynamic interactive spaces to support services to content found behind the portal and also the creation and discussion of new scholarship. In fact, creating a framework to support interaction is a fundamental requirement for scaling not only large-scale content building, such as ongoing institutional repository creation, but also providing avenues for smaller scale interaction within, for example, virtual scholarly communities. Portal frameworks with interactive capabilities will allow for peer review systems, dynamic discussion and vetting of scholarship, and new ways of thinking about the evaluation and preservation of scholarship. It may be that the relatively new "grid community" concept provides this capability. The e-Science Community InfoPortal, for example, is meant to increase user effectiveness by registering information about the e-science virtual organizations with cross searching capabilities.[18] The University of California eScholarship Repository has the tagline "author and reader services for rapid dissemination of scholarship."[19] One section includes interactive publications which are intended to use the power of the technology so that users can travel and interact in a dynamic way. Many virtual communities also use this fuller, more dimensional capability as contrasted by flat one-dimensional text or photographs. Hypertext initially made this possible but now the interactive communication and service elements are coming into play.

Interaction demands some kind of input mechanism so that dialogue, text, images, audio, or other means of communication can be inserted into virtual space. Ideally the self-insertion of scholarship can flow through the scholarly stargate only to come out the other side in a highly searchable and useable format.

THE PHYSICAL DIMENSION OF THE SCHOLARLY STARGATE

Creating, contributing, servicing and applying the digital library content to research and teaching requires physical as well as virtual space. A collaborative and partnership spirit is particularly important in creating the spaces needed to harness the power of the digital library. Innovative spaces are being developed on many campuses where students, faculty, librarians, and technologists create content, digitize it in a variety of formats, and put together multimedia scholarship and presentations. These spaces (instructional and lab-oriented) are also used to apply learning technologies for curriculum development. The successful collaborative physical space for digital work emerges from new partnerships among librarians, technologists, and faculty. A web site featuring examples of best practices for collaborative spaces has been developed by the Coalition for Networked Information in partnership with Dartmouth College.[20] The new digital library creates innovative spaces where expertise, content, and sheer creativity come together in a powerful environment for teaching and learning.

VIRTUAL REFERENCE: THE HUMAN FACTOR

Servicing truly robust and content-rich scholarly portals, digital libraries, or institutional repositories depending on your preferred terminology, requires a link to human expertise one way or another. Virtual interactive reference services are quickly populating the research library landscape and may serve this function as they become more developed. They include e-mail reference and interactive "chat" reference services. Of course it is now supplemented by emerging collaborative and interactive reference services such as OCLC's QuestionPoint. Local libraries set up live online reference services and are also starting to provide multi-institutional collaborative approaches at the regional, national, and international level. Services include filing, tracking, and managing web-delivered questions from patrons, automatic routing of questions to appropriate libraries, identification of library strengths to allow this, and integration of QuestionPoint and other services with alternative service provides and local resources.[21] Many other services exist including homegrown and smaller scale local reference "chat." Robust versions of interactive chat services include the ability to demonstrate searches to "see" what the user is doing and comment.

INTEGRATED SEARCHING SERVICES

A fundamental requirement for the scholarly portal is integrated or cross-searching capability within and beyond an institution's resources. This dynamic functionality is what we are all looking for in portals, digital libraries, and discipline-orientated websites. We want to read about a bluebird, see a bluebird, hear a bluebird, and watch a bluebird fly. We want to be able to obtain more information on the bluebird not owned by our library, get this material delivered as quickly as possible, have it on our course website, and solicit scholarly contributions from experts on the bluebird from our campus and beyond including the capability of publishing peer reviewed material on bluebirds. We want to have dynamic discourse with others interested in bluebirds. We want to effectively manage all of the information we've collected on bluebirds. We want to do this with a single search rather than have to decide in advance which boxes to check off in order to search across collections. We want services to enable us to search across institutions as well as our own collections. We want services to search across web resources as well as so-called library and commercial information resources.

INFORMATION MANAGEMENT AND EFFICIENCY TOOLS

An important aspect of the scholarly portal is the ability for users to effectively manage information gained from the portal for specific uses. Citation capability, indexing, storing, and other knowledge management tools are desired. A dynamic integration of research and teaching management tools is desirable. We need tools to help us to apply the resources we find to our specific projects, to keep track of resources, to integrate different media forms, to capture web resources, and to place them in scholarly research output or teaching/learning objects. We want a seamless and easy way to do all of this.

PORTAL CHALLENGES

Development of portal services carry some significant challenges. How do we scale portal services to handle servicing the kind of complex and voluminous scholarly content out there? Are we ready to reallocate staff to work in this very different virtual environment? The scholarly portal implies going well beyond the boundaries of our physical and virtual libraries as they exist today. Are we going to engage in true collaboration where we might need to think differently about process, content, standards, and other things that seem to be clear in the library world, or will we be content with a more isolationist view where our portal or stargate only leads to certain materials or services we are used to delivering. In other words, will we only go to earthlike planets, and force our users to do the same. Are we ready to work effectively with partners from different professional cultures taking full advantage of their unique expertise or stick to our own kind in portal service development? Are we going after too much–too many services, too much content, and too deep into the scholarly web? Or, are we too thin in our approach? Can we position our portals so users will find them? Even today it is difficult to locate the traditional library on some campus webpages. Is there a service aspect to access or "findability" of portals?

A VISION FOR PORTAL SERVICES: NEXT STEPS

I believe services for the scholarly portal will increase in functionality and reach. True cross searching is on the cusp of reality. Virtual services for individuals, students in individual courses, entire campuses, state and regional consortia, and discipline-based groups will be in place. Interactive spaces will lead to more robust intake systems for publishing, including peer review capabilities as appropriate, and perhaps transform scholarly communication forever. Portals will allow for a diversity of materials because of format and presentation flexibility, and will provide information management services to help users keep track and not lose their way. The stargate will lead to new discoveries but in a more user-friendly way. Portal users will not have to slide down the black hole but go directly to the other side with a familiar look and feel, a familiar frame of reference. And, there will not be only one gate but multiple gates put together for us to enter through and understand what's on the other side. Services of all kind are essential components of the scholarly portal connecting the flat with the deep, the visual with the auditory, the real with the imagination, content with expertise, and individual with community.

NOTES

1. Campbell, Jerry D. 2000 "The case for creating a scholars portal to the web: A white paper." *ARL Bimonthly Newsletter*, Issue 211 (August): http://www.arl.org/newsltr/211/portal.

2. Thomas, Sarah E. 2000 "Abundance, attention, and access: of portals and catalogs." *ARL* Bimonthly Newsletter, Issues 212 (October 2000): http://www.arl.org/newsltr/212.

3. Wetzel, Karen A., Jackson, Mary E. "Portal Functionality Provided by ARL Libraries: Results of an ARL Survey." ARL Bimonthly Report 222 (June 2002). http://www.arl.org/newsltr/222/portalsurvey.html.

4. McBride, James. *The Color of Water: A Black Man's Tribute to His White Mother*. New York: Riverhead Books, 1996.

5. Saha, Avi. "Application Framework for e-business: Portals." developerworks: Web architecture, November 1999. http:www-106.ibm.com/developerworks/library/portals/.

6. Clark, Judith. "Subject Portals," Ariadne, Issue 29. October 2, 2001. http://www.ariadne.ac.uk/issue29/clark/intro.html.

7. Heery, Rachel, Carpenter, Leona, and Day, Michael. "Renardus Project Developments and the Wider Digital Library Context." D-Lib Magazine, 7 (4) April 2001. http://www.dlib.org/dlib/april01/heery/04herry.html.

8. OSTI. Subject Portals. http://www.osti.gov/subjectportals/.

9. Large, Andrew, Beheshti, Jamshid, and Cole, Charles. "Information Architecture for the Web: The IA Matrix Approach to Designing Children's Portals." Journal of the American Society for Information Science and Technology, 53 (10) (August 2002): 831-838.

10. Ghaphery, James. "My Library at Virginia Commonwealth University." D-Lib Magazine 8 (7/8) (July/August 2002). http://www.dlib.org/dlib/july02/ghaphery/07ghaphery.html.

11. Dolphin, Ian, Miller, Paul, and Sherratt, Robert. "Portals, PORTALs Everywhere." Ariadne. Issue 33. www.ariadne.ac.uk/issue33/portals/intro.html.

12. MacLeod, Roddy. "EEVL-ution to a Portal." Ariadne. Issue 31. www.ariadne.ac.uk/issue31/eevl.intro.html.

13. Tochtermann, Klaus. 1996 "A first step toward communication in virtual libraries." *Technical Report. Center for the Study of Digital Libraries. Texas A & M University.* http://www.csdl.tamu.edu/csdl/pubs/klaus/TecRepKlaus.

14. Lougee, Wendy Pradt. "Diffuse Libraries: Emergent Roles for the Research Library in the Digital Age." Perspectives on the Evolving Library. Council on Library Resources. August 2002: 4.

15. University of Iowa Libraries. Bailiwick. http://www.bailiwick.lib.uiowa.edu.

16. Caltech CODA. library.caltech.edu/digital/.

17. The OSU Knowledge Bank Planning Committee. A Proposal for Development of an OSU Knowledge Bank. Final report submitted to the OSU Distance Learning/Continuing Education Committee. June 21, 2002. www.lib.ohio-state.edu/Lib_Info/scholarcom/KBproposal.html.

18. Allan, Rob; Chohan, Dharmesh; Wang, Xiao Dong; McKeown, Mark; Colgrave, John; Dovey, Matthew. "UDDI and WSIL for e-Science." http://esc.dl.ac.uk/InfoPortal/.

19. University of California. "eScholarship: Scholar Led Innovations in Scholarly Communication." http://escholarship.cdlib.org/.

20. Coalition for Networked Information and Dartmouth College. "Collaborative Facilities." www.dartmouth.edu/~collab/index.html.

21. Quint, Barbara. "QuestionPoint Marks New Era in Virtual Reference." *Information Today* 19 (7) (Jul/Aug 2002): 50,54.

The Recombinant Library:
Portals and People

Lorcan Dempsey

A distinctive and legible environment not only offers security but also heightens the potential depth and intensity of human experience.

–Kevin Lynch (quoted by Joseph Rykwert)[1]

The words of things entangle and confuse, said the poet Wallace Stevens, and "portal" is certainly one such word. This is in large part because we do not have a shared sense of the "thing" of which it is the word. Indeed, "portal" is one of the least helpful words we have developed in recent years as we come to terms with the changing information environment in which we research, learn and work.

Of course, this confusion is symptomatic of the early stage of our thinking, and of the natural tendency to reach for answers before we really understand what some of the questions are. What I hope to do here is to discuss some of the current ways in which we are using the word, but I really plan to examine the contexts in which it has been invoked and to say something about them, moving beyond the current portal discussion to think about the general network information environment.

I will proceed in this way: A first section will explore some general issues invoked by the portal discussion. A second section will examine some current library approaches to portal construction, with some focus on architectural

Lorcan Dempsey is Vice President, Research, Online Computer Library Center (OCLC), Dublin, OH (E-mail: DempseyL@oclc.org).
© OCLC. Printed with permission.

[Haworth co-indexing entry note]: "The Recombinant Library: Portals and People." Dempsey, Lorcan. Co-published simultaneously in *Journal of Library Administration* (The Haworth Information Press, an imprint of The Haworth Press, Inc.) Vol. 39, No. 4, 2003, pp. 103-136; and: *Improved Access to Information: Portals, Content Selection, and Digital Information* (ed: Sul H. Lee) The Haworth Information Press, an imprint of The Haworth Press, Inc., 2003, pp. 103-136. Single or multiple copies of this article are available for a fee from The Haworth Document Delivery Service [1-800-HAWORTH, 9:00 a.m. - 5:00 p.m. (EST). E-mail address: docdelivery@haworthpress.com].

http://www.haworthpress.com/web/JLA
Digital Object Identifier: 10.1300/J111v39n04_10

concerns. A third section will return to the broader view, considering briefly some aspects of the information environment in which libraries are working, and saying something about how the library manifests its services in a network space, a network space within which, increasingly, resource and service components need to be flexibly combined to support research and learning experiences. The second section is largely focused on a particular strand of current portal development; the third section looks a little more to the future.

The style of this article reflects its origin in a presentation to the *Improved Access to Library Collections Conference*, organized by the University of Oklahoma Libraries, in Oklahoma City, February 2003. In the main, I have followed the structure of the presentation.

1. INTRODUCTION–THE PORTAL QUESTION

Consider two loose characterizations:

> *An information hub. An entry point to information resources. A density of resources and services on the network. A "portfolio" of resources, potentially customized to specific role or individual interests. An aggregation or collection of resources organized to assist particular categories of users.*

> *How the library mediates the engagement of users and resources in a network environment*

The first is broadly reminiscent of various portal definitions. The "portal" is an entry point to a world of resources, designed to save the user time, to unite him or her with relevant resources, and to encourage maximum use of acquired resources. It may be customized to personal or role interests. Such portals are now much discussed and aspired to.

The second characterization talks about an environment. It is arguable that the major service issue facing libraries at the moment is how to develop a network presence, how to make services available to users at the point in their research or learning activity that makes sense. The current network presence is in early stages; think for a moment of the limited utility of the flat alphabetic lists of electronic resources we present to our users.

Here, I argue that a major reason that the portal discussion is often unsatisfying is that we imagine that the portal is a sufficient response to the issues raised by the second characterization above. It is often imagined that the "portal" answers the question of how the library fruitfully engages the variety of resources and the variety of user needs. At best, however, I argue, the portal is only a partial answer; at worst, it obscures the real question. This is for several reasons. One important one is that the user typically will be served by a variety of network services, by a learning management system and a campus portal, for example. There will in fact be several "hubs" around which he or she articulates network behavior. How does the library portal relate to these other hubs of use? They cannot all, despite their aspirations, be "one-stop shops."[2] In short, a portal–however defined–is not a substitute for a strategy for effective use and management of resources in a network environment; it is a part of it.

I return to these issues more fully in section three. For the moment, here are a couple of examples to think about. First, a screen-shot from a project, DEVIL, at the University of Edinburgh (Figure 1).[3] What this shows is a search box for library resources embedded in a learning management system. The rationale here is that the learning management system is an important "hub" of undergraduate use, and that such a service, bringing the library to the student, better supports learning activity and effective use of library resources. The broad aim of the project is to identify resources of interest to tutors in creating courses, and then provide them with tools to permit dynamic data integration between information resources and courses mediated by Learning Management Systems (WebCT in this case). In fact, behind the scenes there is the cross-searching functionality that is central to many library portal initiatives. In the terminology presented below, the learning management system is a presentation environment for library resources. And the library resources are potentially integrated by a cross-searching "broker" which talks to several databases using the Z39.50 protocol behind the scenes. The broker allows a simple search box to be presented, and then invisibly spreads out the search and consolidates the results.

Second, a screen-shot from the University of Delaware (Figure 2). In common with many others, the University has a campus portal. Again, this is potentially a "hub" in the students' network behavior, a place which brings together a range of administrative and university environment information for convenient access. It is described in this way:[4]

> *Welcome to UD&me, your own "pocket-sized" version of the campus Web. UD&me allows you to view personalized information, from a variety of sources, in one convenient place.*

This is built using the widely used open-source "portal framework," U-portal, which takes an ensemble approach to service construction, allowing several "channels" to be assembled in a customizable way. What this screenshot shows is an example page from a guest account at UD&me. You will see a library "channel" where some information about library resources is embedded.

FIGURE 1

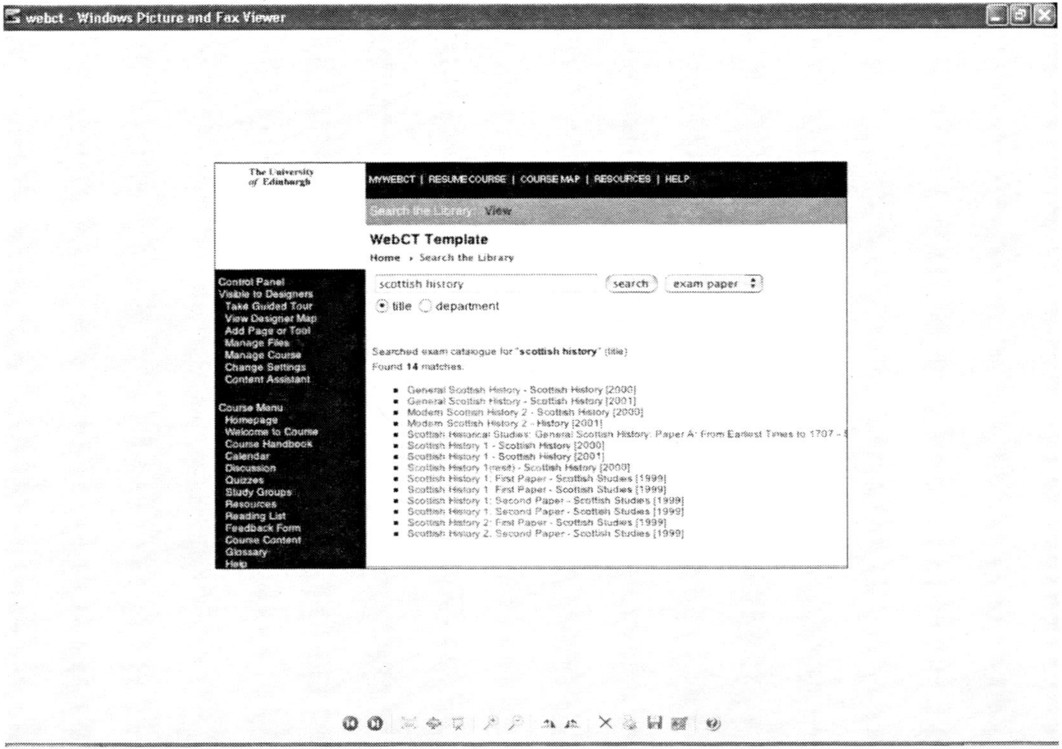

Used with permission.

FIGURE 2

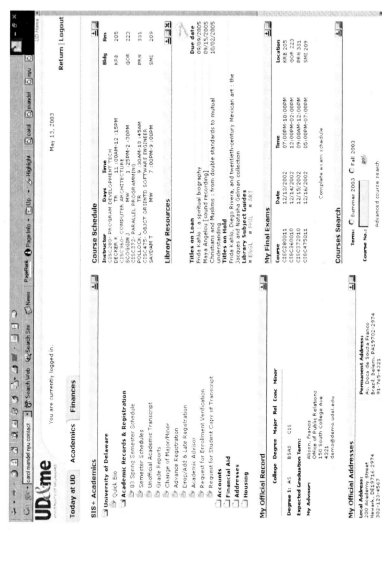

Used with permission.

This includes a note of books checked out, books on hold, and subject resources relevant to the individual's course. So, the library channel is specific to an individual user. Again, a library service is brought to the user, surfaced in an important "hub" alongside other, non-library, resources.

Before moving on, I need to make one very important point about these examples. These are not necessarily substitutes for a library "hub"; they do not replace services provided elsewhere. We are talking "and" not "or": these services may potentially be available in several places, depending on individual or library preference. The important point is that the user–the reader, the learner, the faculty member–has access to a service where it makes most sense. What these examples signal is an "unbundling" of library services so that they can be more readily recombined with other environments to meet service goals.

There is also a third emphasis which is not so readily recognized in the portal discussion, but which is an important one. The library is faced with major issues relating to the management of digital resources; it is not yet a routine issue. Consider for a moment the management of materials in the print library. Librarians have evolved well-understood internal practices and procedures for management, and predictable ways of presenting services for their users. In this, they have been assisted by the evolving technologies of print and publishing, as well as by internal library technologies. Books and journals come in accepted formats, which support some consistency of treatment and arrangement, which allow the advance construction of shelves and processing equipment, the assignment of space, and so on. They only exceptionally require special treatment. These particular technologies have become unobtrusive, experience of them submerged in routine processes. This introduces economies, economies of processing and economies of use. However, digital resources do not always come in this readily processible and presentable form. They often require individual attention, may have different license conditions attached to them, and have different user interfaces. In short they may require custom, and accordingly expensive, treatment. An important strand of the portal discussion is the evolution of an environment which provides a more predictable management context for digital materials, the "shelves" as it were, on which we can routinely line up database offerings. At the moment, the digital environment is one that lacks consistency; it is as if each book coming into the library was a different shape and had to be read in a different way. The benefits of a more consistent environment are clear: library time and resources should be freed to think about selection and use of the collection, not consumed by the messy mechanics of acquisition and processing; and the user experience should be shaped by learning and research needs not by the arbitrary constraints of interface and format. We need to achieve the economies of consistent treatment as well as the benefits of consistent access. The focus in this article is on access, but it is useful to remember that this is part of a larger management issue.

So, let me summarize briefly before moving on to a slightly more detailed discussion of existing portal approaches.

The library wants to provide a web environment which: enriches learning and research by providing timely, convenient access to relevant and appropriate resources; surfaces potentially valuable resources which otherwise might be overlooked; and enables users and the library to focus on fruitful use of collections rather than on the messy mechanics of interaction. Such environments increasingly need to interact with other environments such as the learning management system, institutional portal frameworks, and the other "hubs" of network presence. I suggest that this means that the current portal discussion marks a transitional phase. The question we need to address is not the integration of library resources with each other; it is the integration of library services with the learning and research behaviors of users. The former may sometimes be a means to achieve the latter, however it should not be confused with it.

2. A SCHEMATIC REVIEW OF CURRENT LIBRARY PORTAL APPROACHES[5]

In this section, I will provide a framework for thinking about the "portal" response in libraries. There have been two main strands in this response. The first of these is to provide cross-searching or metasearch services, services which basically allow one to treat a "portfolio" of resources as if they were one by providing a "meta" service which hides their difference and which searches across them and combines the results. These have been the focus of considerable research and development activity, and are now supported in a variety of products and services. (In recent work by the Association of Research Libraries a "portal" is defined as an application providing a metasearch service and one other supporting service.[6]) The second is to provide "views" of sets of resources based on individual or role preferences. In each case, the main focus has been on access to bibliographic resources, catalogs, abstracting and indexing services, e-journals, and locally developed databases, as well as on access to openly available Internet resources. Of course, some applications provide both of these service components.

On the Perceived Need and Historical Development of Library Portals

Figure 3 represents the network information environment as it has historically developed. A user typically interacts with a range of information resources. The introduction of the Web may have provided a consistently navigable overlay on this environment, but the following issues remained.

FIGURE 3

Portal Issue

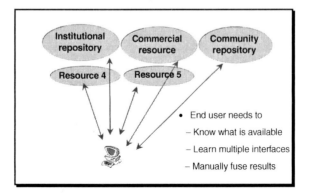

The user had to:

- *Know what is available.* To use a resource, the library user typically has to know in advance of its existence. Of course libraries get around this by developing lists of resources, but these are not always the most effective way of guiding users to resources of potential interest. *This issue has driven an interest in personalization and customization, as a way of fruitfully matching users and resources.*
- *Learn multiple interfaces.* Typically, a user has to "learn" each resource. They may have different features, different interaction metaphors, different combinations of functionality. This variety is a disincentive to use. The motivation to use information resources has to overcome the barrier caused by this variety. *This has driven an interest in cross-searching activity, where a user interacts with a range of resources through a higher level interface which hides difference.* (Interestingly, I think that one of the impacts of Google and Amazon has been to move towards much more streamlined interfaces with some commonality.)
- *Manually fuse results or move data between applications.* Typically, resources are available at user interfaces not at machine interfaces, and resources are not linked to each other. What this means is that a user will have to fuse results themselves, for example, aggregating various result sets into a bibliography, or will often have to take data from one system, a catalog, for example, and re-enter it in another, an Interlibrary Loan system, for example. Of course there may be integration within particular

system environments, an integrated library system, say, but moving data out of that environment is not always easy. Accordingly, "integration" tends to happen at the user level: the user manually manipulates results and requests. Furthermore, it means that the data is often less useful than it should be, because its structure is thrown away when it is delivered at a user interface; it cannot be reused intelligently. Again, these issues have been an impediment to most effective use. *This has driven an interest in consistency of metadata and development of agreed machine interfaces.*

- *Meet repeated authentication challenges.* To carry out a simple procedure–to search in several databases, for example–a user may have to remember and enter several sets of credentials. *This has driven an interest in distributed approaches to authentication and authorization.*

At the same time, resources tended to be developed as if each were the sole focus of a user's attention, rather than as a part of the fabric of service provision. This has led to some particular resource characteristics:

- *A provider view.* They are organized by supplier interests, rather than by scholarly or pedagogical value or user preference. Resources are often grouped by publisher or aggregator, which rarely maps onto user interest.
- *Autonomous.* They are autonomously managed; they have developed independently, responsive to different service and business goals. This means that within any information process, it may be necessary to interact with several services which do not coordinate their activities. So, for example, there are network services which accept document requests, there are packages which can format requests for dispatch to such services, there are services which allow people to discover the documents of use to them. These may not be linked in such a way that an end-to-end process can be automated. Data may not cross boundaries, or may have to be re-keyed or transcribed by user or by staff. This issue has recently been highlighted and is driving an interest in identifiers and linking, which help to automate discovery to delivery chains.
- *Individually controlled.* Information providers wish to protect the value of resources they make available. They will almost definitely make resources available under different terms and conditions. There may be a need to confirm the identity of users or the integrity of resources. At present identity, access, and rights management services are provided on a service-by-service basis, creating significant impediments to use.
- *Different functional aggregation.* For example, a journal aggregator may allow people to discover, request and have delivered a particular selection of journal articles from a particular selection of publishers. An ab-

stracting and indexing service allows users to discover the existence of documents. Some services may be offered as "one stop shops." Although some organizations now offer services which include discover, locate, request and deliver facilities, they are still just components within this potentially distributed document supply service since no server will meet all coverage or quality of service criteria.

- *Limited disclosure of content*. They say little about themselves to a potential user. Services require the user to have significant advance knowledge of what is available, and some persistence if they wish to use several resources.

Together these issues reduce the motivation to use the resources provided by libraries; this is not to say that they are not valuable, rather that they are difficult to use.

Contrast this situation with Amazon and Google. Each of these is immediately accessible on the Web (no need to remember a password), gives the appearance of being comprehensive within their areas (no apparent need to prospect multiple different resources), and offers instant gratification (click through to a web-site or a purchase).

The library portal response to these issues is to provide some intermediate layers between users and resources. These aim to overcome the fragmentation of the resources, and to provide a unified interface which reflects a user interest rather than the arbitrary characteristics of format, interaction or delivery channel.

Figure 4 shows this in a schematic way.

On Some Important Portal Distinctions

In considering the nature of this "intermediation" it is crucial to grasp some important distinctions. Again, our current lexicon does not give us much help, always a sign of early development.

Let us define a *service* simply as a functional component available on the network. There is then a major qualitative distinction between two types of service, which is crucial in characterizing portal approaches. This is one between resources provided at user interfaces and those provided at machine interfaces.

In the first case, a resource is made available at, say, a web page. The intended consumer is a human, so it is oriented towards reading and navigation. Integration of resource content needs to be provided by the user. Think of the user who successively looks at several catalogs: typically, he or she will have to manually integrate, sift, manipulate or merge. Most of our information services are now made available in this way. Think of the library "portal" which provides organized lists of Internet resources. The user may be guided to re-

FIGURE 4

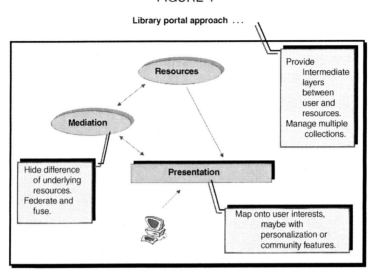

Library portal approach ...

Resources

Mediation

Presentation

Provide Intermediate layers between user and resources. Manage multiple collections.

Hide difference of underlying resources. Federate and fuse.

Map onto user interests, maybe with personalization or community features.

sources of interest, but once they commit to looking at a particular resource, they leave the "portal" environment and are delivered to the door of the remote resource. Think of lists of e-journals, or of abstracting and indexing databases: again, the user may be guided, may have a personalized list of resources presented to them, but is then delivered to the front door of the desired resource. Once they go through the door of the desired resource, the user is in that remote resource environment, and needs to behave appropriately. The desired resource sits on the network behind its own user interface. Integration is shallow. For convenience, I refer to services which appear at a user interface as p-services, where "p" stands for "presentation" and "people": "p" services are oriented towards presentation and are aimed at people.

As Figure 5 illustrates, a p-portal provides an entry-point to p-services. So, we could describe the access lists mentioned above as p-portals. A database of resource descriptions could also be considered as supporting a p-portal, as would a personalisable environment like MyLibrary. The key thing is that a p-portal does not itself shield the user from the differences of the target resources, or link them together.

In the second case, a resource is made available at a machine interface, and the expected consumer is not a human but a program, a machine. So, for example, a service may disclose resource metadata for harvesting by an OAI-PMH-

FIGURE 5

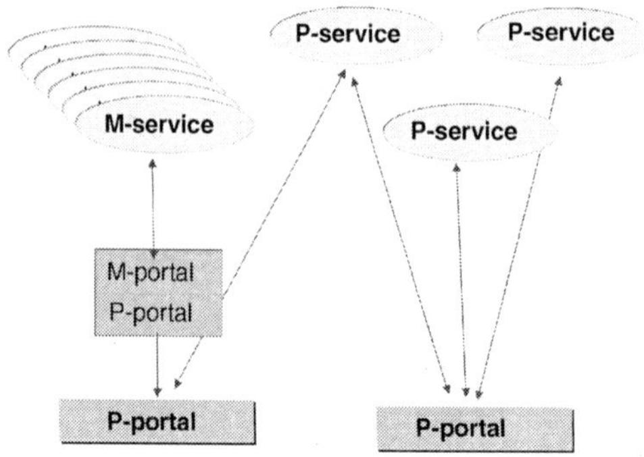

compliant harvester, or for search by a Z39.50 client. In each case, the service must support a protocol (OAI-PMH or Z39.50, respectively) and a machine interface which can interact with the consuming application.

We could name a service available at a machine interface an m-service. And an m-portal provides access over m-services–"m" here stands for "machine" and "mediation," the latter because the m-portal does not just deliver a user to the door of a service, it reaches into the remote resource on the user's behalf. In this case, the key issue is that the user does not leave the m-portal environment: an m-portal application goes out and interacts with services on the user's behalf. A better word than m-portal might be "broker," or portal application. A broker provides a deeper level of integration. Here are examples of what broker applications do:

- Hide difference and the mechanics of interaction from users, so as to save time and simplify procedures. An example here would be a cross-searching application which creates a federated resource from several others. Of course, such applications raise various complications in implementation.
- Facilitate flow of data between applications so as to automate processes. This includes inter-application integration. An example here would be a resource sharing application which mediates searching, ILL, resolution, and document delivery transactions, perhaps interfacing with billing or other applications.
- Aggregate resources for further use. An example here would be an OAI-PMH-based harvester which takes data from several sources and makes it available at a machine or a user interface. The Open Archives Initiative Protocol for Metadata Harvesting is a technique for sharing metadata between services. One service–a data provider in OAI terms–makes metadata

available in an agreed way; another service comes and "harvests" it. The latter service–a service provider in OAI terms–may harvest from multiple "data providers" and in turn may provide access to the metadata it collects in this way.

The crucial thing, then, about mediation, in this conversation, is that it involves the orchestration of machine-to-machine interactions which allow a higher level of abstraction to be introduced between the user and the resources. This in turn has an important further consequence: it means that resources have to be made available at machine interfaces. (The focus here has been on bibliographic resources, typically metadata resources. Increasingly, as I discuss in part 3, libraries will provide access to a richer range of resources.)

Of course, the distinction between m-services and p-services is becoming blurred. Nevertheless, in the current environment there is an important distinction to be made, particularly when it comes to complexity and cost of implementation. We have limited broker or mediation services in current library environments, and the reasons include their cost of implementation, the burden placed on resource operators to support additional protocols or processing, and some concern about effectiveness in the current network environment. Of course, mediation and presentation services are not exclusive. Typically mediation services support presentation: services will be delivered at some stage to a user interface.

And the distinction may become even more blurred as the Web becomes more application rich. Syndication using RSS (Really Simple Syndication) is a good example here. The emergence of 'web services' is also very important. "Web services" is the phrase introduced by the World Wide Web Consortium to denote a suite of protocols that define how requests and responses between software applications should be encoded and transferred over the Web. I discuss this approach further below.

This distinction allows us to further discriminate between current library portal developments, as in Figure 6. This shows four quadrants characterized by whether they provide mediation in addition to presentation and by whether they are customizable to individual or role interests, or are static. Here are some observations on candidates for each quadrant:

1. mediation/static. An example would be one of the commercial library metasearch products which does not profile by user.
2. mediation/customizable. An example would be one of the commercial library metasearch products which includes the ability to profile by user.
3. presentation/static. This might be a list of links on a university gateway. There are many such resources. An elaboration might be a database of descriptions of such resources. A subject gateway provides an example here.[7]

4. presentation/customizable. An example here is MyLibrary, "a user-driven, customizable interface to collections of Internet resources–a portal." An application, "primarily designed for libraries, *the system's purpose is to reduce information overload* by allowing patrons to select as little or as much information as they so desire for their personal pages."[8]

I include this characterization because of what seems to me to be a confusion in discussion between these groupings, which in turn rests on a confusion between portals which aggregate what I have called p-services and those which aggregate m-services.

On Portal Services–An Architectural Perspective

I now want to turn to the question of what types of services are being provided through portals, and some scalability and architectural issues that are beginning to emerge based on experiences to date.

Figure 7 shows a range of candidate services for a portal. Some of these will be available in some portals. Some portals will provide services that are not listed here.

- *Distributed query or "metasearch."* This is a central component of library portal offerings. Typically, a broker will search across several target databases. There are a variety of approaches: Z39.50, custom query techniques, and various inelegant screen-scraping techniques. Z39.50 is now well established and its strengths and weaknesses well understood. There are many issues surrounding indexing practice, different controlled vocabularies and so on. More recently, there has been an interest in new approaches which preserve some of the semantics of Z39.50 but implement them as "web services." These go by the names of SRW and SRU.[9] Distributed query approaches are supported in several scenarios where a library wants to offer a search across several databases. This may be to group disciplinary abstracting and indexing services; it may be to search across a group of library catalogs; it may be to bring together different resource types to give a unified experience.
- *Harvesting.* A more recent approach looks at bringing metadata together by harvesting–a program, a broker, collects metadata from several sites. This metadata can then be made available for searching. The Open Archives Initiative Protocol for Metadata Harvesting provides a mechanism for managing the relationship between the harvested and harvesting sites. To date, we have seen little production use of OAI-PMH, but its wider deployment is much anticipated.
- *Syndication.* I use this term to refer to the increasingly common use of RSS. RSS (a contested acronym, here expanded as Really Simple Syndi-

cation) is an XML-based format for sharing content between web applications; it is typically used to embed or aggregate feeds of structured data, news for instance. RSS is being used by many people to share alerts, updates or other structured lists of current information.[10]

- *Request.* A portal application may allow a document or other resource to be requested, through circulation, ILL or other application.
- *Deliver.* It may allow receipt of a document or other resource.
- *Configuration.* I am using configuration as a summary label for an especially interesting set of issues. For a portal effectively to mediate between user interests and available resources it will need to "understand" quite a bit about the environment, both about users and resources. First of all, it will need to be able to talk to a variety of machine interfaces. Even if it only talks Z39.50 it will have to know something about the configuration of each target database: what port it is at, what record formats or services are supported, and so on. If it talks to a variety of target databases with custom machine interfaces, or if special programs have to be written to interact with them, then other data may need to be held. We can call this data "service description." It is also common to store some data which says something about the databases or collections available, which can be used to pop up some descriptive text on a user interface, or which can be searched by a user looking for relevant resources. This type of data is sometimes known as "collection description," although of course that term has a wider sense to include structured description of library and other collections.[11] To support customization, a portal may need to know something about a user, something about their privileges, maybe something about their preferences or their past behavior. In each of these cases, it may not be unusual to configure the portal application itself with this data. However, it also makes sense to interact with external directories, and in some cases, it may make sense to share this data across applications or institutions. Certainly, in a campus environment, for example, one would want to avoid duplicating user data. Library portals are currently redundantly creating service and collection descriptions. Anecdotal evidence suggests that this is a significant burden for the portal manager, or system supplier where it takes on this role: it is an interesting question as to whether third party services which removed the burden of individual data creation would be feasible.
- *Personalization.*[12] Many services have personalization components, typically local to the system itself. They may be based on historic use or stated preferences, as suggested above. A simple personalization approach would be to match user profiles against collection descriptions, or to allow a user to select from a checklist.

- *Reference.* There is considerable recent interest in virtual reference–the mortal in the portal–where access is provided to a local or distributed human reference resource.[13]
- *Annotation.* This is a user-oriented application, were users or groups of users might be able to add sharable or local annotations to a resource.
- *Notification.* Again, this is a user-oriented service which provides alerts about some matter of interest, about, for example, new or changed resources. Syndication would be one means of providing this service.
- *Terminology service.* Such services are not widely deployed but we may expect them to become more common, whether offered directly to a user, or provided in the background interacting with a programmatic user carrying out a search. Examples of services which might be useful: map between controlled vocabularies, enrich query terms with associated terms, associate personal or corporate names with names matched from an authority file, expand acronyms, associate synonyms, broaden or narrow the search by moving within a thesaural hierarchy, and so on. Again, these types of services, where they are available, have been integral with a particular search service; they could also be externally provided.
- *Resolution.* A resolution service will typically take an identifier and return data about the resource identified. In the last couple of years a particular type of resolution service, based on the OpenURL, has become very important in library portal applications. An OpenURL provides a way of encoding citation data and exchanging it between services. Reference linking applications have emerged which are configured so as to resolve an OpenURL in a way that is configurable to the particular context of the user. So, in a typical scenario, given a journal article, a user might be directed to the local collection, to a particular aggregator, and so on. This is a way of linking metadata for a resource with the "appropriate" copy of that resource, as determined by the library.
- *Result enrichment and fusion.* A cross searching application will often merge results from different sources, sometimes deduplicating them. However, it may also be possible to enrich data from a third party. So, for example, a search service may consolidate catalog records from several sources, and it may enrich those records with table of contents data pulled from a third party on the fly.
- *Rights management.* Particular terms and conditions will be associated with resources. Increasingly, libraries are having to manage multiple licenses.
- *Identity management.* This is another complex area. A major application area for portals is to provide single sign-on, so that a user is not repeatedly challenged as they move between services. In this context, a user needs to be authenticated (to establish that they are who they purport to be), and then authorized to use particular services.

FIGURE 6

A portal grid!

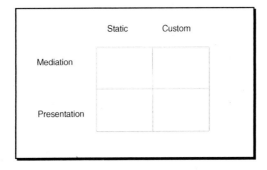

FIGURE 7

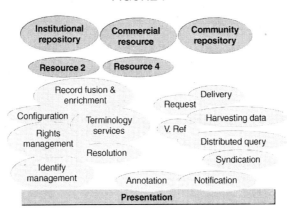

Few portals incorporate this range; some portals may have other services. In the current model, services tend to be specific to the portal. However, a moment's reflection shows that many of these services are potentially common to several applications within an organization, or across organizations.

So, for example, many services on a campus will want to authenticate users. If we think of portal applications across several similar institutions, it is likely that there is some overlap in the collection or service description that they create: there is redundant and costly local configuration effort. Some other examples were mentioned earlier. Thinking along these lines prompts us to think again about separating the described services into categories. Figure 8 provides a distinction between services which are potentially common to many applications and the applications which provide the portal functionality.

This is further elaborated and slightly abstracted in Figure 9. The portal may need access to data about institutions, collections, services, rights, and policies (think about a portal that provides resource sharing services–one may want access to information about library ILL policies). Potentially, the portal may want access to intelligence about all of the objects of interest to it in directory-type services. The portal may require access to resolution services which are potentially shared with other applications. Similarly for terminology services, and crucially for identity management services.

What we see emerging is a situation where, potentially, the portal not only interacts with a range of information resources to support the user, but also interacts with a range of common services which allow it to do its job more effectively or cheaply. It will be interesting to see if the incentives to work in this way are strong enough to see the emergence of such shared services.

Finally, a note on metasearch applications. Although, there is now a lot of experience in using such applications, we don't appear to have a settled consensus on their role and usefulness. It is likely that research libraries, and potentially others, will use them to provide sensible aggregations (by subject, level or course, for example). However, they may also want to provide access to the target resources themselves for those with more particular interests. For a brief but judicious appraisal see the recent article by Roy Tennant.[14]

FIGURE 8

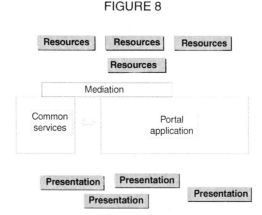

FIGURE 9

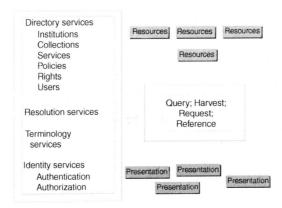

Some Summary Remarks on Part 2

Part 2 has discussed the library portal, focusing on current capability and the bibliographic environment. Here are some summary observations based on this discussion:

- The library portal as conceived in recent years provides intermediation between a fragmented resource base and a view of an "information landscape" adapted to user interest.
- The level of intermediation may vary. A crucial distinction can be made between portals which provide integration at the presentation level only, and those which provide richer mediation at machine interface level. The former involve bringing together a set of resources, maybe with single sign-on, personalization or other user services, but not taking the user beyond the front door of the target resources. They remain individual opportunities. The user may be guided, but still has to drive the use of target information resources. The latter involve the use of mediating applications or brokers to weave target resources into a higher level application which shields the user from their underlying difference. Here the user drives an application, and it is the application which drives a set of other services. Various products exist to assist in portal construction in each case.
- The range of services offered by portals is wide, and growing. Some of these services are common, in that they are potentially used by other services whether within the same institution (authentication, for example) or

across institutions (service description directories, for example). It would seem to make sense not to build these services redundantly portal by portal, and it will be interesting to see whether incentives are strong enough to lead to a market of third party or shared services to meet these needs.

- The recognition that there may be common services across portals, the desire to provide services in various presentation environments, and the growing interest in "web services" to provide modular building blocks, move one to an architectural perspective in which one can identify services and their relationship at a more fine-grained level. This is an important topic in Part 3 below.

My opening discussion focused on "information resources," reflecting the initial primary interest on providing access to digital resources. The natural tendency now is to begin to talk about "services" as the environment becomes richer. Some services make resources available; some facilitate the environment of information use.

3. MEDIATING THE ENGAGEMENT BETWEEN RESOURCES AND USERS

Locations, Collections and Services

The library might be seen as an articulation of three components: a location, a collection of resources, and a set of services (using services in a broad sense here). Historically, these three components coincided in the physical space of the library and the library as functional entity involved collocation of library users, library collections and library staff. This co-incidence continues to create value for library users. However, we are also seeing the separation of these three components in a network environment, and their co-development in a new constellation of mutual interaction. In this final part, I want to use a discussion of these three components as a way of thinking about access in a network environment.

Thinking About Locations and Hubs

In considering the impact of the network on place, William Mitchell[15] observes:

> *We will, I believe, plot our actions and allocate our resources within the framework of a new economy of presence. In conducting our daily transactions we will find ourselves constantly consulting the benefits of the different grades of presence that are now available to us, and weighing these against the costs.*

So, interestingly, as collections and services move to the network, we see a renewed emphasis on the library place as "agora," as a social assembly space. Developments include major new building work which focuses on this social aspect and on the symbolic aspect of the library, a growing interest in the exhibition and display of special collections and rare materials, on redeveloping space for social learning and interaction, on the library as a neutral "third place," and on information and research commons activities.

At the same time, in the emerging library economy of presence, users look for library services in other locations. In one view of it, the "library portal" is an aspiration to create *the* library service location on the Web; just as library users may once have found their way to the physical library building, now, the thinking goes, they will find their way to the library portal.

However, consider for a moment what is happening, for example, in a university context.[16] There is likely to be a university-wide portal initiative, which aims to bring together a range of administrative and university data, perhaps with single sign-on and some personalization. Typically, in the terms presented earlier, this is a p-portal over data from various university agencies. There also may be–in a more or less coordinated fashion–an investment in a learning management system. In each case, the service provides a "hub," potentially another portal. And there may be other internal hubs, emerging digital lab-book environments, for instance, or departmental sites. And certainly, there will be external hubs of use: Google, disciplinary resources, ResearchIndex, and so on. Against this background, the aspiration to create the "one-stop-shop" for information needs seems a forlorn hope. The user will potentially interact with a variety of hubs.

Thinking About Collections

The grid[17] presented in Figure 10 is a schematic way of considering collection development attention. There are two axes: "stewardship" and "uniqueness." The binary divide is a stylization, used for its mnemonic qualities only–each axis is a spectrum. The grid also provides a snapshot in time, and, in fact, one of its uses–not explored here–is to consider how materials might move in line with developing trends. It was developed to show how different forms of material call forward different forms of attention, and here it is used to prompt a brief discussion of changing patterns of access.

By "stewardship" we wish to suggest the degree of curatorial attention that materials receive by libraries. Highly stewarded materials are collected, organized, preserved. Thus, "left of the line," materials tend to be in library collections, and subject to traditional practices of organization and access. By "uniqueness" we wish to suggest the degree to which materials exist in more

FIGURE 10

Collections grid!

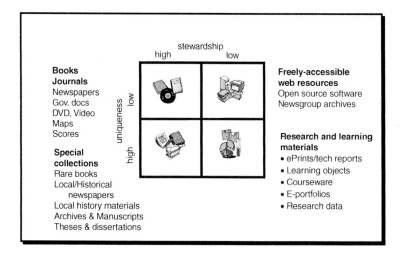

than one collection. Thus, "below the line," objects or collections are unique or rare, are currently relatively inaccessible, and tend to be institutional assets rather than more widely published materials.

Consider briefly some issues arising from each quadrant:

1. *Upper left. Formally published materials (books, journals, DVDs, videos, etc.).* These materials tend to exist in many collections; to be supported by a well-developed apparatus of catalogs and union catalogs, and abstracting and indexing services; to be published in multiple copies and possibly available in multiple versions. Materials are either licensed (typically digital materials–journals and indexes) or bought (books, videos, etc.). Much of the library portal activity has focused in this area, and some of the particular issues that have emerged (reference linking and the appropriate copy problem, for example, or resource sharing applications) flow from the specific publication characteristics of these materials and the apparatus of their provision. There is an articulation of catalogs for discovery and location of materials (union catalogs at national, state or regional levels; distributed resource sharing arrangements) and an interlibrary loan apparatus in place to request items. Much portal activity focuses on cross-searching the abstracting and indexing resource, the electronic journal resource, and articulating these and the book resource.

Much of the focus here is internal to the institution (interacting with its licensed materials), or, where external, flows through well understood, if evolving, organizational arrangements (for resource sharing/ILL).

2. *Lower left. Unique and rare materials in library collections. Special collections, archives and manuscripts.* There is growing appreciation among libraries that unique or rare materials are valuable research and learning resources, that they have been underutilized, that digitization offers opportunities for releasing their value in new ways. There is a growing interest in digitizing cultural heritage materials, as a way of disclosing the memory and identity of communities. Many research libraries have archives departments and are creating finding aids. This has led to increased interest in how to make their resources available on the network, and some interest in approaches based on harvesting of metadata. Some of this material is available in library catalogs, much is not. It presents issues of description (sometimes hierarchical approaches using EAD or other techniques, sometimes Dublin Core based item level description, sometimes unitary collection level description). In terms of access, there is interest in using OAI-PMH to aggregate metadata for this material, and some of it is represented in existing catalogs and union catalogs. However, there remain large aggregation and discovery issues. An interesting and unresolved issue relates to the articulation of collections and items in discovery scenarios. In libraries we are used to providing access at the item level. We don't yet have widely agreed ways of characterizing collections. We have little experience of thinking about providing access at different levels of granularity and aggregation in digital environments. How do you move interestingly between descriptions of collections and items?

3. *Lower right. Research and learning materials.* Research and learning behaviors are increasingly network mediated. There is growing investment in learning management systems to mediate and manage the learning experience. Learning materials are being produced in various digital forms, and learning technology is being introduced in different ways in different environments. The library may be more or less involved, depending on local circumstances. There are at least two broad areas of engagement: involvement in the life cycle management of learning materials (creation, description, management, discovery, use and reuse), and interaction between systems environments. The latter is increasingly important for the academic library: library resources and services need to be accessible within the learning management environment.

Research activity is similarly diffuse. Faculty may use computational, information or communication resources on the network. Increasingly, research results are available, in "raw" form or as a part of broader resource such as an exhibition or learning materials. There are curated data sets across disciplinary areas. There is a movement to make e-prints available as part of the open access movement.[18] In these and other cases, the library is emerging as a potential partner, as a source of expertise, as a persistent institutional venue which provides continuity of management and economies of scale. Recently, the term "institutional repository"[19] has emerged as a general summary label for a range of supporting services the library might offer in this environment, working with faculty to provide curatorial attention to a dispersed, complex resource. An important aspect of this activity is organized disclosure of institutional informational assets using the Open Archives Initiative Protocol for Metadata Harvesting.

4. *Upper right: Wide open Web.*[20] Libraries have taken several approaches to selecting and organizing materials on the Web for their users, from simple pages of links to reasonably full description. This effort has been massively redundant across libraries. The "subject gateway" is one interesting response.[21] Of course, most users discover resources here using Google or other search engines, and this again raises an interesting question about the focus of library activity. Should library resources be disclosed in a way that they are indexed by Google and thereby rendered potentially discoverable by Google? In the coming years how much of the materials in the other quadrants will be indexed by Google and with what implication for other forms of access? Of course, discovery is but one service that a library provides, and I argue below that the library service experience on the network needs to be much enriched.

What can we say about access and portals in the light of this stylizing analysis? As libraries look forward, a major issue becomes providing access to a whole range of material, but a variety of issues will need to be worked through:

- *Above and below the line.* Library portal activity initially has been focused "above the line," on providing access to catalog and journal data, and to some extent on providing access to Internet resources. The focus is bringing together materials for a local population. As already noted, the library community has established and developing options for discovery and delivery of their book collections. They are working with others on a rapidly developing apparatus to provide access to the journal literature. However, the situation "below the line" is much less mature. Some material surfaces in catalogs. But there is a growing resource whose fragmentation across organizations makes discovery difficult. There are many "puddles" of data which are not brought together in any critical mass. Currently there is a focus on harvesting data, but sustainable production models have not developed. This makes it potentially difficult for any individual library to provide access to the wide range of special collections materials across other institutions.

- *To the left and right of the line.* Materials on the left are generally "library" materials; they are procured and managed by the library. This is not the case to the right of the line. There, there may be various levels of library involvement. For example, within universities, Wendy Lougee has spoken about a model of "collection federation" where the library may not have control over individual collections but may provide a larger federating service which provides unified access to collections which continue to be autonomously and externally managed.[22] She cites the example of the University of Michigan's Image Service in this context, and notes that such directions involve complex balancing of roles between the library and the collection manager. As we look at developments in learning management and at nascent institutional repository discussions,[23] it is clear again that libraries, in some cases, are beginning to put in place models for such activity, but that no single pattern is emerging. This is within institutions. Again, when one looks across institutions the aggregation of such materials is in very early stages.

- *A unified pattern?* What this means is that there is not a unified pattern of activity across the quadrants. There are well-developed, though changing, activities in the upper left quadrant. New approaches are being developed in the others. This complicates provision, within and between institutions. It is interesting to consider a technical example here. What acronyms does one associate with the upper left quadrant? Perhaps MARC21, Onix (used in the book industry), OpenURL (increasingly important for tying together services), DOI (used by publishers), Z39.50. What about below the line? Here the picture is much more diffuse. Perhaps Dublin Core, EAD, OAI, IEEE/LOM, and then a host of community- and discipline-specific approaches. The different forms of attention that the quadrants receive complicates the provision of integrated access. There are different metadata schema, many ways of organizing subjects, and so on.

This analysis suggests that the range of library attention will grow to embrace the development of a variable set of services across materials with quite different characteristics.

Thinking About Services

It is sometimes suggested that content is king, that the major imperative of digital initiatives is to make collections available. But this is to ignore the relationship advanced at the beginning of Part 3 between location, collections and services. Appropriate services make collections come alive. Our emerging network information environments are still limited: we have limited instruments to do interesting things with collections, to make associations, to manipulate and analyze content or metadata, to repackage, to navigate. Current portal environments tend to allow us to discover, locate, request and deliver resources. These are broad, general services, which only bring the user some way along the path of effective information use.

In this section, I briefly look at two examples of how services might better work to support user behavior. These are taken from research work on humanities scholars, and from current discussion about libraries and learning management systems. Then I look at some implications of a "service ensemble" model.

Developing Services: The Example of Humanities Scholars

Here I want to point to the work of Carole Palmer and colleagues in exploring the behaviors of interdisciplinary humanities scholars.[24] She identifies a variety of patterns. These include a desire to prospect a contextual mass of literature (not just the top scholarly journals or the canon), iterative reading of a personal collection of texts, wide reading and chaining (collections created by citation links and bibliographies), collection communities, rich finding aids that cross institutions and fields of studies.

A moment's thought shows how current digital environments could do much more to support some of these behaviors. For example, the current dominant discovery experience in portal environments is searching or browsing databases or lists of references. It would be useful to allow people to enter an information space through annual reviews of the literature or review articles, or by following citation chains, or to traverse richly associated resources.[25] (The popularity of ResearchIndex is interesting.) We provide limited support for the creation of personal collections.

This is a small example of the limited instruments we have in digital environments to support use and users. It is important to remember this, and to remember that richer services are key to making users more "at home" in the digital environment.

Developing Services: The Example of Libraries and Learning Management Systems

The DEVIL example earlier showed how a search service could be embedded in the learning management system. However, it is clear that there are a range of other services that could be useful surfaced in this way. These include the ability to be able to consistently link to resources, to be able to search repositories, to be able to request items from services, to be able to interact with virtual reference systems, to be able to manipulate digital assets for incorporation in learning materials, and so on.

Building these types of links make sense, but also raises difficult and subtle issues. Consider briefly, for example, the question of reading lists. These are a place where library and learning management interests intersect. What requirements might one have of a reading list builder? To be able to take citations from different databases and add them to a single structured document? Exchange that document easily between applications (e.g., between a learning management system and a library portal application) and between authors while retaining its structure? So that a faculty member could create a list, and a librarian could add some general resources, maybe linking it to other library resources, and pass it back again? Include "canned searches" against particular databases or combinations of databases? Have persistent links to remote licensed resources? Be able to include and share annotations? Resolve citations against an OpenURL resolver to ensure that the appropriate copy of a resource is obtained? Integrate with authentication and authorization services. These are all sensible things to do. However, what seems to be emerging is a view of the reading list as a sharable portal, with all the attendant issues we have discussed above.

Again, the structures to provide this level of integration are in early stages of development. But it is this articulation of fine-grained services which will allow the library to create value for the learning process by supporting the user at point of need.

Articulating an Ensemble of Services–Environments and Architectures

Two broad directions are emerging: richer services which support and develop alongside research and learning behaviors, and more fine-grained services which can be woven into multiple environments flexibly.

What might all this mean? I think that these directions have major implications for how the library provides its services, which we are only beginning to investigate.

The first direction suggests a much more thorough exploration than hitherto of the range of service that it is appropriate to provide. This will proceed in a bottom-up way, based on local experiment, curiosity and imagination. At some stage though, this will develop into some consensus about what services a library provides and how. The second involves thinking about granularity, interoperability, design and related issues. Each involves a deep engagement with users and partners, a diffusion of interests, along the lines discussed by Wendy Lougee.[26] How will the library co-evolve with research, learning and general information use?

Each direction also moves us towards an architectural perspective, a seemingly inevitable consequence of service unbundling and reconfiguration. An architecture is a mechanism for agreeing the components of an environment and the relationship between them. The advantage of architecture is that it focuses a discussion. It provides a common framework for design, discussion, or planning. It allows you to partition a problem. One of the confusions of the library portal discussion is that it proceeds without a shared architectural context which grounds it in a shared understanding.

Take two recent examples of service architectures. The JISC Information Environment looks at how a set of national UK services might be developed in concert.[27] Effectively, it describes an environment onto which a portal provides a view. Another service architecture has been developed by IMS, the organization which coordinates specification work within the learning management community. It has developed a Digital Repository Interoperability framework to frame discussion and development about how learning management systems and repositories communicate to create higher level services.[28] Effectively, this again provides a view of how a portal (in this case provided by the learning management system) fits into a wider environment of services. At a high level these architectural initiatives are quite similar; they discuss similar services and seek to facilitate similar types of design and discussion.[29]

A second major factor in the "service" discussion is the emergence of "web services." Web services are defined by the World Wide Web Consortium as:

> *The World Wide Web is more and more used for application to application communication. The programmatic interfaces made available are referred to as web services.*[30]

Web services are modular applications available on the Web. They may be recombined to provide other services. Effectively, they seek to create a framework for easily combining distributed applications. Google and Amazon make interfaces available as web services so that others can more easily build them into their applications. I mentioned SRW above; this is a recasting of Z39.50 as a web service. This is not the place to discuss web services in any detail; however, it is important to note that they provide a framework for developing and deploying "m-services" more easily.

Finally, in this section, I want to mention "portal frameworks." I have already mentioned u-portal. U-portal is an example of a portal framework, an application that allows you to tie together various services in a presentation-oriented "portal" service. Effectively, services become "channels" or "portlets" in a user-configurable environment. There are several commercial and open-source portal framework applications available. It is interesting to see the library discussion intersect with a general industry concern to standardize here.[31]

So, to bring together some of this discussion: should the library create its own hub in network space, or is it better to appear elsewhere, to surface services in other hubs? Hitherto, in the short history of network information systems, the former has been the preferred option; gradually we will probably see the latter emerge more strongly as it is supported by technology and driven by the need to be available in the research and learning workspace. Remember the examples given in the opening section: the surfacing of modular library services in the university portal, and the library management system at the Universities of Delaware and Edinburgh, respectively.

However, given the discussion in this section, maybe this divide is not so great as it first seems. Each direction moves to a similar architectural conclusion: the modularization of services so that they can be recombined as occasion demands, whether brought together in a library hub or portal, or embedded in other hubs. The technology discussed here may facilitate this trend, but is not essential to it. This recombinance will increasingly be the hallmark of network information services. And clearly, to recapitulate the discussion in Part 2, each of these hubs may increasingly draw on common services. Figure 11 begins to show this. A range of hubs draw on common services, and also selectively on library services.

Such an environment raises major issues for the way in which the library is visible to its users; it raises major issues about identity and perception of value. It brings us back to my opening remarks: the major development issue facing libraries today is how to create a network environment which is rich in services and which meshes with user behavior in useful and convenient ways.

Some Summary Remarks on Part 3

Early portal activity focused on a small set of services over a range of well-understood resources. The focus was on the discovery process. Metasearching and customized presentation of resources were, and are, popular services. However, a range of new issues emerge as location, collections and services are separated in a network environment, and co-evolve with user behavior, itself evolving:

- *Locations.* The library needs to integrate information resources with the research and learning lives of their users. The integration of library resources in a "library hub" is one approach, however, increasingly libraries are interested in "projecting" their services to other hubs also. This means that it is increasingly important to be able to provide a richer set of services in a fine-grained way. The physical library itself is being reconfigured to emphasize the social, the face-to-face, and the special.

- *Collections.* The collections landscape is becoming more complex. Libraries are providing support over a range of differently managed collections. These may be collections of metadata or collections of metadata and content, they may be curated within the library, or outside of the library, they may deploy different metadata and knowledge organization approaches, they are a mix of common and special. The library is interested in providing access to external resources. Many libraries are also increasingly interested in making more of their own resources, and the resources of their home institutions, available to external users. This, in turn, touches on major questions about future patterns of information use and scholarly communication.
- *Services.* To create viable digital information environments the library will need richer services, provided more flexibly, in ways that can be woven into user behavior more easily. This, in turn, prompts some unbundling of services, and a greater interest in architectural issues and emerging "web services" approaches.

The issues raised here are complex, and will take time to work through. My purpose has been to show that the network information environment goes beyond our current portal thinking in interesting ways, ways which will require major work to address.

CONCLUSION

In this article I have discussed the emergence of "library portals," network hubs which bring together users and resources of interest to them. I have noted how such portals have become richer, embracing a wider set of services. I have suggested that our current portals mark a transitional phase as we look towards the creation of network environments that mediate the engagement of users and information resources. Users may benefit from a library hub, but they will also benefit from integration of appropriate resources into their research, learning and information use behaviors in more fine-grained and particular ways. This means that we are beginning to see an unbundling of library services so that they can be better recombined with other environments, such as learning management systems or campus portals. Such an unbundling, in turn, means that architectural issues become more important, especially as we begin to explore what services are needed to support effective network presence and the institutional and organizational frameworks through which they are provided.

The reconfiguration of presence and the mutual influence of physical place and network place has led to a heightened perception of the social aspect of li-

FIGURE 11

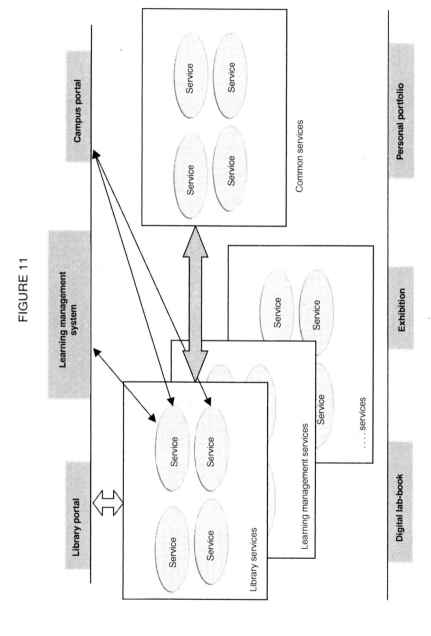

brary places, their role as a "third place," as learning exchanges, as venues for collaboration and display.

At the same time, the library is looking at working with a collections environment in which it is mediating access to bought and licensed resources, to common and unique materials, to institutional resources which may or may not be in the libraries' curatorial care. It is looking to create new structures within which cultural heritage and research and learning materials are brought together across institutions for creative use. It is looking at how it manages this range in an integrated way, and what services will make these collections visible and valuable.

We are still in the early stages of thinking about what all of this means for the library and for the services it provides. The portal is part of a picture, but we need to look beyond it to build and sustain the services which enter the fabric of our users' research, learning and informational experiences.

REFERENCES

1. Rykwert, Joseph. The seduction of place. New York: Vintage Books, 2002.
2. "One stop shop" is another unhelpful phrase we use. A "one stop shop" is in fact a "one shop stop."
3. Edinburgh University. DEVIL project [website]. http://srv1.mvm.ed.ac.uk/devilweb/ (checked 8 June 2003). (Thanks to John MacColl for sharing the screenshot with me.)
4. University of Delaware. *UD&me* [website]. http://uportal.udel.edu/student/ (checked 8 June 2003). (Thanks to Gregg Silvis for drawing this to my attention.)
5. This section draws on a variety of sources.

Lorcan Dempsey. The library, the catalogue, the broker. *New Review of Information Networking*, Volume 5, 1999. (Also available in: *Information landscapes and a learning society: networking and the future of libraries 3*. Sally Criddle, Lorcan Dempsey, Richard Heseltine, eds. London: Library Association Publishing, 1999.) (Also available at http://www.ukoln.ac.uk/dlis/models/publications/landscape/ (checked 9 June 2003))

Lorcan Dempsey, Rosemary Russell and Robin Murray. A utopian place of criticism?: brokering access to network information. *Journal of Documentation*, 55(1), 1999, 33-70. (Also available at http://www.ukoln.ac.uk/dlis/models/publications/utopia/ (checked 9 June 2003))

6. ARL: Access and Technology Program: Scholars Portal. *Portal functionality provided by ARL libraries: preliminary results of an ARL survey*. April 11, 2002. http://arl.cni.org/access/scholarsportal/prelim.html (checked 9 June 2003).
7. Dempsey, Lorcan. The subject gateway: experiences and issues based on the emergence of the Resource Discovery Network. *Online Information Review*, Vol. 24, No. 1, April 2000, pp. 8-23. (Also available at http://www.rdn.ac.uk/publications/ior-2000-02-dempsey/ (checked 9 June 2003))
8. Morgan, Eric Lease. *MyLibrary* [website]. http://dewey.library.nd.edu/mylibrary/. (checked 8 June 2003).

9. Library of Congress. *ZING: Z39.50 international: next generation.* [website] http://www.loc.gov/z3950/agency/zing/srw (checked 9 June 2003).

10. Pilgrim, Mark. What is RSS? *O'Reilly XML.com* [website]. http://www.xml.com/pub/a/2002/12/18/dive-into-xml.html (checked 9 June 2003).

11. Powell, Andy; Heaney, Michael; Dempsey, Lorcan. RSLP collection description. D-Lib Magazine. Vol. 6, No. 9, 2000. http://www.dlib.org/dlib/september00/powell/09powell.html (checked 9 June 2003).

12. See for examples of current approaches and research directions: *Proceedings of the Second DELOS Network of Excellence Workshop on Personalisation and Recommender Systems in Digital Libraries: ERCIM Workshop Proceedings-No. 01/W03* [website]. Sponsored by the U.S. National Science Foundation, Dublin City University, Ireland, 18-20 June 2001. http://www.ercim.org/publication/ws-proceedings/DelNoe02/ (checked 9 June 2003). There is a succinct keynote by Clifford Lynch, Personalization and Recommender Systems in the Larger Context: New Directions and Research Questions, http://www.ercim.org/publication/ws-proceedings/DelNoe02/CliffordLynch Abstract.pdf.

13. See the special issue of *D-Lib Magazine* in February 2003 on digital reference for a good overview of this developing area. http://www.dlib.org/dlib/february03/02contents.html.

14. Tennant, Roy. The right solution: federated search tools. *Library Journal*, 6/15/2003. http://libraryjournal.reviewsnews.com/index.asp?layout=article&articleid=CA 302427&display=Digital+LibrariesNews&industry=Digital+Libraries&industryid=%industry id%&verticalid=151 (checked 30 June 2003).

15. Mitchell, William J. E-topia. Cambridge, MA: MIT Press, 2000.

16. The range of interest is nicely captured in the program and accompanying presentations at: *Portals 2002: an institutional imperative.* A conference jointly hosted by the University of Nottingham and JISC, June 7 2002. http://www.nottingham.ac.uk/portals2002/programme.htm [website] (checked 9 June 2003). This includes presentations about U.S. and UK enterprise portals, and a general discussion of electronic information environments.

17. This grid was initially developed by Lorcan Dempsey and Eric Childress in the context of internal OCLC discussions. It is further explored in a series of presentations by Dempsey which can be found at www.oclc.org/research/staff/dempsey/presentations.shtm.

A recent ARL presentation gives a fuller treatment: Dempsey, Lorcan. Place and space: Collections and access in light of changing patterns of research and learning: a schematic view. *A community commons: libraries in the new century*: ARL proceedings of the 142nd annual meeting, Lexington, Kentucky, May 14-17, 2003. www.arl.org/arl/proceedings/142/dempsey.html.

18. The focus here is on how the library creates access environments for its users. It should be noted in passing that these developments raise major questions for the library role and its support for changing patterns of scholarly communication and access which are not discussed here.

19. SPARC. Institutional repositories [website]. http://www.arl.org/sparc/core/index.asp?page=m0 (checked 9 June 2003).

20. This material is characterized as non-unique here as it is can potentially be added to many collections, it is routinely cached, and sometimes archived.

21. Dempsey, Lorcan. The subject gateway: experiences and issues based on the emergence of the Resource Discovery Network. *Online Information Review*, Vol. 24,

No. 1, April 2000, pp. 8-23. (Also available at http://www.rdn.ac.uk/publications/ior-2000-02-dempsey/ (checked 9 June 2003))

22. Lougee, Wendy Pradt. Diffuse libaries emergent roles for the research library in the digital age. Washington, DC: Council on Library and Information Resources, 2002. (Also available at http://www.clir.org/pubs/reports/pub108/contents.html (checked 9 June 2003))

23. Lynch, Clifford A. Institutional repositories: essential infrastructure for scholarship in the digital age. *ARL Bimonthly Report*, February 2003. http://www.arl.org/newsltr/226/ir.html (checked 12 June 2003).

24. See the publication and presentation list at http://www.lis.uiuc.edu/~clpalmer/pubspres.html. In particular see Palmer, Carole L. and Laura Neumann. The Information Work of Interdisciplinary Humanities Scholars: Exploration and Translation. *Library Quarterly* 72, 2002, p. 85-117.

25. See, for example, the experimental prototype FictionFinder from OCLC Research which allows you to traverse associations created between genres, characters, imaginary places, and real places. http://fictionfinder.oclc.org/.

26. Lougee. Op cit.

27. UKOLN. JISC Information Environment. [website]. http://www.ukoln.ac.uk/distributed-systems/jisc-ie/arch/ (checked 9 June 2003).

28. IMS. IMS Digital Repositories Interoperability–Core Functions Information Model Version 1.0 Final Specification. (Revision 13 January 2003) http://www.imsproject.org/digitalrepositories/driv1p0/imsdri_infov1p0.html (checked 30 June 2003).

29. The approaches are compared by Andy Powell in a presentation given at the CETIS Metadata and Digital Repository Interoperability SIG, Milton Keynes, December 2002. *IMS Digital Repositories Interoperability* http://www.ukoln.ac.uk/distributed-systems/jisc-ie/arch/presentations/cetis-mdrsig-2002-12/ (checked 9 June 2003).

30. W3C. *Web services activity*. http://www.w3.org/2002/ws/ (checked 9 June 2003).

31. OASIS. Web Services for Remote Portlets Specification Committee Specification 1.0, 6 July 2003. http://www.oasis-open.org/committees/download.php/2750/wsrp-specification-1.0-cs-1.0-rev1.doc (checked 5 July 2003). (OASIS is an industry standards group. This document specifies how a portal framework interacts with web services.)

Index

© 2003 by The Haworth Press, Inc. All rights reserved.

Access, Ownership, and Resource Sharing, edited by Sul H. Lee (Vol. 20, No. 1, 1995). *The contributing authors present a useful and informative look at the current status of information provision and some of the challenges the subject presents.*

Libraries as User-Centered Organizations: Imperatives for Organizational Change, edited by Meredith A. Butler (Vol. 19, No. 3/4, 1994). *"Presents a very timely and well-organized discussion of major trends and influences causing organizational changes." (Science Books & Films)*

Declining Acquisitions Budgets: Allocation, Collection Development and Impact Communication, edited by Sul H. Lee (Vol. 19, No. 2, 1994). *"Expert and provocative. . . . Presents many ways of looking at library budget deterioration and responses to it . . . There is much food for thought here." (Library Resources & Technical Services)*

The Role and Future of Special Collections in Research Libraries: British and American Perspectives, edited by Sul H. Lee (Vol. 19, No. 1, 1993). *"A provocative but informative read for library users, academic administrators, and private sponsors." (International Journal of Information and Library Research)*

Catalysts for Change: Managing Libraries in the 1990s, edited by Gisela M. von Dran, DPA, MLS, and Jennifer Cargill, MSLS, MSEd (Vol. 18, No. 3/4, 1994). *"A useful collection of articles which focuses on the need for librarians to employ enlightened management practices in order to adapt to and thrive in the rapidly changing information environment." (Australian Library Review)*

Integrating Total Quality Management in a Library Setting, edited by Susan Jurow, MLS, and Susan B. Barnard, MLS (Vol. 18, No. 1/2, 1993). *"Especially valuable are the librarian experiences that directly relate to real concerns about TQM. Recommended for all professional reading collections." (Library Journal)*

Leadership in Academic Libraries: Proceedings of the W. Porter Kellam Conference, The University of Georgia, May 7, 1991, edited by William Gray Potter (Vol. 17, No. 4, 1993). *"Will be of interest to those concerned with the history of American academic libraries." (Australian Library Review)*

Collection Assessment and Acquisitions Budgets, edited by Sul H. Lee (Vol. 17, No. 2, 1993). *Contains timely information about the assessment of academic library collections and the relationship of collection assessment to acquisition budgets.*

Developing Library Staff for the 21st Century, edited by Maureen Sullivan (Vol. 17, No. 1, 1992). *"I found myself enthralled with this highly readable publication. It is one of those rare compilations that manages to successfully integrate current general management operational thinking in the context of academic library management." (Bimonthly Review of Law Books)*

Vendor Evaluation and Acquisition Budgets, edited by Sul H. Lee (Vol. 16, No. 3, 1992). *"The title doesn't do justice to the true scope of this excellent collection of papers delivered at the sixth annual conference on library acquisitions sponsored by the University of Oklahoma Libraries." (Kent K. Hendrickson, BS, MALS, Dean of Libraries, University of Nebraska-Lincoln)* Find insightful discussions on the impact of rising costs on library budgets and management in this groundbreaking book.

The Management of Library and Information Studies Education, edited by Herman L. Totten, PhD, MLS (Vol. 16, No. 1/2, 1992). *"Offers something of interest to everyone connected with LIS education–the undergraduate contemplating a master's degree, the doctoral student struggling with courses and career choices, the new faculty member aghast at conflicting responsibilities, the experienced but stressed LIS professor, and directors of LIS Schools." (Education Libraries)*

Library Management in the Information Technology Environment: Issues, Policies, and Practice for Administrators, edited by Brice G. Hobrock, PhD, MLS (Vol. 15, No. 3/4, 1992). *"A road map to identify some of the alternative routes to the electronic library." (Stephen Rollins, Associate Dean for Library Services, General Library, University of New Mexico)*

Managing Technical Services in the 90's, edited by Drew Racine (Vol. 15, No. 1/2, 1991).
"Presents an eclectic overview of the challenges currently facing all library technical services efforts. . . . Recommended to library administrators and interested practitioners." (Library Journal)

Budgets for Acquisitions: Strategies for Serials, Monographs, and Electronic Formats, edited by Sul H. Lee (Vol. 14, No. 3, 1991). *"Much more than a series of handy tips for the careful shopper. This [book] is a most useful one–well-informed, thought-provoking, and authoritative." (Australian Library Review)*

Creative Planning for Library Administration: Leadership for the Future, edited by Kent Hendrickson, MALS (Vol. 14, No. 2, 1991). *"Provides some essential information on the planning process, and the mix of opinions and methodologies, as well as examples relevant to every library manager, resulting in a very readable foray into a topic too long avoided by many of us." (Canadian Library Journal)*

Strategic Planning in Higher Education: Implementing New Roles for the Academic Library, edited by James F. Williams, II, MLS (Vol. 13, No. 3/4, 1991). *"A welcome addition to the sparse literature on strategic planning in university libraries. Academic librarians considering strategic planning for their libraries will learn a great deal from this work." (Canadian Library Journal)*

Personnel Administration in an Automated Environment, edited by Philip E. Leinbach, MLS (Vol. 13, No. 1/2, 1990). *"An interesting and worthwhile volume, recommended to university library administrators and to others interested in thought-provoking discussion of the personnel implications of automation." (Canadian Library Journal)*

Library Development: A Future Imperative, edited by Dwight F. Burlingame, PhD (Vol. 12, No. 4, 1990). *"This volume provides an excellent overview of fundraising with special application to libraries. . . . A useful book that is highly recommended for all libraries." (Library Journal)*

Library Material Costs and Access to Information, edited by Sul H. Lee (Vol. 12, No. 3, 1991). *"A cohesive treatment of the issue. Although the book's contributors possess a research library perspective, the data and the ideas presented are of interest and benefit to the entire profession, especially academic librarians." (Library Resources and Technical Services)*

Training Issues and Strategies in Libraries, edited by Paul M. Gherman, MALS, and Frances O. Painter, MLS, MBA (Vol. 12, No. 2, 1990). *"There are . . . useful chapters, all by different authors, each with a preliminary summary of the content–a device that saves much time in deciding whether to read the whole chapter or merely skim through it. Many of the chapters are essentially practical without too much emphasis on theory. This book is a good investment." (Library Association Record)*

Library Education and Employer Expectations, edited by E. Dale Cluff, PhD, MLS (Vol. 11, No. 3/4, 1990). *"Useful to library-school students and faculty interested in employment problems and employer perspectives. Librarians concerned with recruitment practices will also be interested." (Information Technology and Libraries)*

Managing Public Libraries in the 21st Century, edited by Pat Woodrum, MLS (Vol. 11, No. 1/2, 1989). *"A broad-based collection of topics that explores the management problems and possibilities public libraries will be facing in the 21st century." (Robert Swisher, PhD, Director, School of Library and Information Studies, University of Oklahoma)*

Human Resources Management in Libraries, edited by Gisela M. Webb, MLS, MPA (Vol. 10, No. 4, 1989). *"Thought provoking and enjoyable reading. . . . Provides valuable insights for the effective information manager." (Special Libraries)*

Creativity, Innovation, and Entrepreneurship in Libraries, edited by Donald E. Riggs, EdD, MLS (Vol. 10, No. 2/3, 1989). *"The volume is well worth reading as a whole. . . . There is very little repetition, and it should stimulate thought." (Australian Library Review)*

The Impact of Rising Costs of Serials and Monographs on Library Services and Programs, edited by Sul H. Lee (Vol. 10, No. 1, 1989). *". . . Sul Lee hit a winner here." (Serials Review)*

Computing, Electronic Publishing, and Information Technology: Their Impact on Academic Libraries, edited by Robin N. Downes (Vol. 9, No. 4, 1989). *"For a relatively short and easily digestible discussion of these issues, this book can be recommended, not only to those in academic libraries, but also to those in similar types of library or information unit, and to academics and educators in the field."* (*Journal of Documentation*)

Library Management and Technical Services: The Changing Role of Technical Services in Library Organizations, edited by Jennifer Cargill, MSLS, MSed (Vol. 9, No. 1, 1988). *"As a practical and instructive guide to issues such as automation, personnel matters, education, management techniques and liaison with other services, senior library managers with a sincere interest in evaluating the role of their technical services should find this a timely publication."* (*Library Association Record*)

Management Issues in the Networking Environment, edited by Edward R. Johnson, PhD (Vol. 8, No. 3/4, 1989). *"Particularly useful for librarians/information specialists contemplating establishing a local network."* (*Australian Library Review*)

Acquisitions, Budgets, and Material Costs: Issues and Approaches, edited by Sul H. Lee (Supp. #2, 1988). *"The advice of these library practitioners is sensible and their insights illuminating for librarians in academic libraries."* (*American Reference Books Annual*)

Pricing and Costs of Monographs and Serials: National and International Issues, edited by Sul H. Lee (Supp. #l, 1987). *"Eminently readable. There is a good balance of chapters on serials and monographs and the perspective of suppliers, publishers, and library practitioners are presented. A book well worth reading."* (*Australasian College Libraries*)

Legal Issues for Library and Information Managers, edited by William Z. Nasri, JD, PhD (Vol. 7, No. 4, 1987). *"Useful to any librarian looking for protection or wondering where responsibilities end and liabilities begin. Recommended."* (*Academic Library Book Review*)

Archives and Library Administration: Divergent Traditions and Common Concerns, edited by Lawrence J. McCrank, PhD, MLS (Vol. 7, No. 2/3, 1986). *"A forward-looking view of archives and libraries. . . . Recommend[ed] to students, teachers, and practitioners alike of archival and library science. It is readable, thought-provoking, and provides a summary of the major areas of divergence and convergence."* (*Association of Canadian Map Libraries and Archives*)

Excellence in Library Management, edited by Charlotte Georgi, MLS, and Robert Bellanti, MLS, MBA (Vol. 6, No. 3, 1985). *"Most beneficial for library administrators . . . for anyone interested in either library/information science or management."* (*Special Libraries*)

Marketing and the Library, edited by Gary T. Ford (Vol. 4, No. 4, 1984). *Discover the latest methods for more effective information dissemination and learn to develop successful programs for specific target areas.*

Finance Planning for Libraries, edited by Murray S. Martin (Vol. 3, No. 3/4, 1983). *Stresses the need for libraries to weed out expenditures which do not contribute to their basic role–the collection and organization of information–when planning where and when to spend money.*

Planning for Library Services: A Guide to Utilizing Planning Methods for Library Management, edited by Charles R. McClure, PhD (Vol. 2, No. 3/4, 1982). *"Should be read by anyone who is involved in planning processes of libraries–certainly by every administrator of a library or system."* (*American Reference Books Annual*)

SPECIAL 25%-OFF DISCOUNT!

Order a copy of this book with this form or online at:
http://www.haworthpress.com/store/product.asp?sku=5166
Use Sale Code BOF25 in the online bookshop to receive 25% off!

Improved Access to Information
Portals, Content Selection, and Digital Information

_____ in softbound at $18.71 (regularly $24.95) (ISBN: 0-7890-2445-4)
_____ in hardbound at $29.96 (regularly $39.95) (ISBN: 0-7890-2444-6)

COST OF BOOKS _____ Outside USA/ Canada/ Mexico: Add 20%. _____ **POSTAGE & HANDLING** _____ US: $4.00 for first book & $1.50 for each additional book Outside US: $5.00 for first book & $2.00 for each additional book. **SUBTOTAL** _____ In Canada: add 7% GST. _____ **STATE TAX** _____ CA, IL, IN, MIN, NY, OH, & SD residents please add appropriate local sales tax. **FINAL TOTAL** _____ If paying in Canadian funds, convert using the current exchange rate. UNESCO coupons welcome.	❑ **BILL ME LATER:** Bill-me option is good on US/Canada/ Mexico orders only; not good to jobbers, wholesalers, or subscription agencies. ❑ **Signature** _____ ❑ **Payment Enclosed: $** _____ ❑ **PLEASE CHARGE TO MY CREDIT CARD:** ❑ Visa ❑ MasterCard ❑ AmEx ❑ Discover ❑ Diner's Club ❑ Eurocard ❑ JCB **Account #** _____ **Exp Date** _____ **Signature** _____ *(Prices in US dollars and subject to change without notice.)*

PLEASE PRINT ALL INFORMATION OR ATTACH YOUR BUSINESS CARD

Name		
Address		
City	State/Province	Zip/Postal Code
Country		
Tel	Fax	
E-Mail		

May we use your e-mail address for confirmations and other types of information? ❑Yes ❑No
We appreciate receiving your e-mail address. Haworth would like to e-mail special discount
offers to you, as a preferred customer. **We will never share, rent, or exchange your e-mail
address.** We regard such actions as an invasion of your privacy.

Order From Your Local Bookstore or Directly From
The Haworth Press, Inc.
10 Alice Street, Binghamton, New York 13904-1580 • USA
Call Our toll-free number (1-800-429-6784) / Outside US/Canada: (607) 722-5857
Fax: 1-800-895-0582 / Outside US/Canada: (607) 771-0012
E-Mail your order to us: Orders@haworthpress.com

Please Photocopy this form for your personal use.
www.HaworthPress.com

BOF04

JWML LIBRARY
P.O. Box 98
1 College Drive
Lame Deer, MT 59043

Reference Only
Not to be removed
from Library.